FULLNESS OF JESUS

CHRISTIAN LIFE IN THE NEW TESTAMENT

Tabernacle Sermons - II

BY

Rev. A. B. SIMPSON

PASTOR GOSPEL TABERNACLE, NEW YORK.

Originally Published By:

NEW YORK:
THE WORD, WORK AND WORLD PUBLISHING COMPANY,
Madison Avenue and Forty-fifth Street.

Vol. 2 Tabernacle Sermons
Sermons preached from May – September, 1886,
at Tabernacle on Madison Ave. and 45th Street.
Printed December, 1886

Authored by A. B. Simpson

Republished under Public Domain rights by:

Empowered Publications Inc.

529 County Road 31

Millry, Al 36558

ISBN: 978-1-943033-20-1

Tabernacle Sermons

Beginning in 1886 A.B. Simpson began publishing a series of books called "Tabernacle Sermons." These books contained messages that he had preached in the Gospel Tabernacle, New York City, New York and subsequently published in eleven volumes.

These books are reprints of their original volumes. The content has been kept as close to the original as possible. Spelling was modernized in a few places, and where there were obvious errors in the text (one or two), comparisons were made to later editions of the books to keep the author's intent. Some of the original eleven volumes were combined, and some of the author's other books were added into the series.

VOLUME 1
The King's Business

VOLUME 2
The Fullness Of Jesus

VOLUME 3
The Gospel Of The Kingdom

VOLUME 4
Natural Emblems Of Spiritual Life

VOLUME 5
In Christ

Containing Three Volumes: The Four-Fold Gospel, The Christ Life, & The Christ Life And The Self Life (This book was originally printed as three separate books: The Four-Fold Gospel, Volume 5 of Tabernacle Sermons; The Christ Life, Volume 8 of Tabernacle Sermons; and The Christ Life And The Self Life, which was printed as an individual book.)

These three small volumes were combined as their contents relate to each other, and also to give the reader the most content for their purchase.

VOLUME 6
Divine Emblems In Genesis And Exodus

(This book was originally printed as two separate volumes: Volume 6, and Volume 7, in the original Tabernacle Sermons.)

VOLUME 7
Christ In The Tabernacle And Leviticus

(This book was originally printed as two separate books Volume 9 Christ in the Tabernacle – part of the Tabernacle Sermons Series; and Christ in Leviticus – part of the Christ in the Bible Series.)

VOLUME 8
Joshua & The Land Of Promise

(This book was originally printed as two separate books: The Land Of Promise Volume 10 of Tabernacle Sermons; and Christ in Joshua – part of the Christ in the Bible Series.

VOLUME 9
Walking In The Spirit &
When The Comforter Came

(This book was originally printed as two separate books: "Walking In The Spirit," Volume 11 of Tabernacle Sermons, and "When The Comforter Came" was printed as a thirty-one day devotional dealing with the Holy Spirit.

CONTENTS.

CHRIST RAISING THE DAUGHTER OF JAIRUS.

CHRIST KNOCKING.

CHAPTER I.

THE FULNESS OF CHRIST

"And I am sure that, when I shall come unto you, I shall come in the fulness of the blessing of the Gospel of Christ." – Rom. 15:29

I.

*T*HE first word in this text is blessing. It comes to us laden with all the memories of Christ's first word on earth, and His last look as He left the world. The Old Testament ended with the word curse, and the sermon on the mount began with blessed. And, as He parted from them and was carried into Heaven, His hands were extended in blessing as they looked upon Him for the last time until He should come again. And so, this morning as we enter this place, we find those hands are over us still, and we believe those lips are still saying: "Blessed are the poor in spirit, blessed are they that mourn, blessed are the meek, blessed are they that hunger and thirst, blessed are the merciful, blessed are the pure in heart, blessed are the peacemakers blessed are they that are persecuted for righteousness' sake."

The idea that we always associate with blessing is quite different. When you think of the blessings that you are thanking Him for today, I am not so sure that you are thinking of poverty of spirit. I am afraid your mind is on the circumstances of your life, on your homes, your friends, your children, your business, your possessions; but God's blessing is for the poor in spirit—them that mourn, them that hunger. O may we come with that spirit into this new period of our work. If we do, we need not ask to be blessed, for we are already blessed and the cloud has fallen on our heads. And if the last stage of the blessing should be suffering, we should not shrink even from that, nor fear to drink the cup of the Master, which has such a blessed reversion by and by when we shall drink the new wine with Him in the kingdom.

May He add to us the more blessed, which is to give rather than to receive, and make it our highest blessedness here not to be seeking blessings, but to be a blessing.

This is the word that He gave to Abraham when He sent him out. "I will bless thee; be thou a blessing." So God speaks this word BLESSING today. May God speak it to you all through the coming years, and may it be said of us: "Blessed are the people that know the joyful sound, they shall walk in the light of Thy countenance. Blessed is the man whom Thou choosest and causest to approach unto Thee. Blessed are they that are called to the marriage supper of the Lamb." For I do believe God is calling us forth for His Coming and to that highest blessing when He shall gather us to His own bosom, to His own table, in His own kingdom.

II.

Then the second word is "Christ"—"the fulness of the blessing of Christ." There is another reading of this passage which many of you are familiar with, and it is a very slight change from the present version, but makes an immense difference in the meaning—"The blessing of Christ," instead of "The blessing of the Gospel of Christ." Even the Gospel must not come between us and Christ Himself. An old painter made such an excellent painting of the Last Supper that his critics, when they came to view it, saw only the beauty of the cups. They did not even notice the face of the Saviour, and he felt that he had failed. And I might so preach to you the Gospel that you would think only of the ideas and the truths, and you would not see the living one Himself. The blessing Christ wants to give us is the blessing of which Christ is the substance and the soul.

Were I to ask you, this morning, what is the most blessed thing in your life, humanly speaking, I don't think you would say it is your business; I don't think you would say it is your house; I don't think you would say it is even your pleasure; I think every true heart would say; "The people that I love." What would that mother take for her child? Would she take a house or a million dollars for its precious life and love? No; it is worth more than everything else. There is scarcely a man or woman here this morning who would not, if I asked them the question, say: "Somebody that I love is dearer to me than everything in the world about me." A living person, then, is the most blessed thing of my life and of your life. I am sure that is the true answer of every heart here today. And so it is in the divine life. It must be a living person there if it is to satisfy. It must be the Christ and not the gifts of the Christ, not the things He can do or can give, but the love that He has for you and that He gives to you.

Beloved, is the Christ as real and as dear to you as the friend you love. You would not give up all else for this dear one of earth? Would you give up Christ for this dear one? O, you must say: "I love Thee more than all these."

Now, a great many don't see these blessings as they are centerd in Him. They want to get the blessing of salvation, but that is not the Christ. They want to get the blessing of His grace to help, but that is not Him. They want to get answered prayer from Him to work for Him. You might have all that and not have the Blessing of Christ Himself. A great many people are attached rather to the system of doctrine. They say: "Yes, I have got the truth; I am orthodox." That is not the Christ. It may be the cold statue in the fountain with the water passing from the cold hands and lips, but no life there. A great many other people want to get the blessing of joy, but that is not the blessing of Christ personally. A great many people are more attached to their church and their pastor, or to dear Christian friends, but that is not the Christ. The blessing that will alone fill your heart when all else fails, is the loving heart of Jesus united to you, the fountain of all your blessings and the unfailing one when they all wither and are exhausted—Jesus Christ Himself.

O, beloved, have you this blessing of the Christ? Can you say: "I have got Him; I have got His loving presence in my heart. There is a Man that stands beside me that I know as I know nobody else. There is a living reality in my heart that is better than all I am. I have Him who is the First and the Last. Something has been born within me that is the Son of God. Christ has come to dwell in me. He makes my being part of the divine nature. There is a secret whisper in my heart that I know comes from Him. There is a gentle touch upon my soul that I know is the finger of God. Jesus is mine; Jesus is within me. My God in the midst of me is mighty."

> "Fade, fade each earthly Joy,
> Jesus is mine."

May the Lord make you and me know HIM, the power of His resurrection and His living presence, if you don't know it. Oh, may He make this known not only as the Church of the Disciples, proper as that name is. May it be the house where Jesus' name is written on every wall and on every face. Yes, it is blessed, not merely to be pardoned, not merely to be strengthened in body, not merely to be in-dwelt, but just to know Him as we know nobody else, to love Him as we love nobody else, to have

Him as well as His gifts, and to be waiting for His coming with a longing desire which can never rest, and then to know that as He is, so am I in this world; that all that belongs to Him belongs to me; that I can pray in His name as He would pray; I can do all things through Christ that strengthens me; I cannot be a separate self from Him, not I, but Christ liveth in me. And when I think of the other world, I cannot think of being separate there.

> "For Jesus has loved me, I cannot tell why;
> But this I can find—we two are so joined,
> That He'd not be in glory and leave me behind."

There is a story told of an old Norwegian king that once was given a drinking horn to drink from, and he began to drink it all up; but, as he kept on drinking, it seemed as if it never would empty. When he got tired, he looked around and found that it was connected with a pipe, and that the pipe was connected with the ocean, and that as fast as the horn emptied the water ran in and filled it, and that he would have to drink up the whole ocean in order to empty the cup. The reason so many are not satisfied is that they haven't got the ocean back of their cup; and, O, if you get Christ behind you, He is a spring of everlasting life. You cannot drink it dry any more than you can drink the ocean dry. And, so, we determine to know nothing among you but Jesus Christ. We want you to see no man, exalt no man, forget every human power, and every human authority and every human voice that does not rest on Christ's Word. We bring to you Jesus; we bring, perhaps, the fulness of Jesus in some way you have not seen before, but it is all Him. If there is to be more joy in your heart, it is to be the joy of Jesus; if there is to be more power in your life, it is to be Jesus; if there is to be more strength in your body, it is because you are closer to the Lord.

III.

The next word is the word "sure." How many people in the world are tormented about things they are not sure about! What a miserable thing it is when you cease to be sure of the love of your friends. What a risk businesses is when men are not sure of their securities. A break in public confidence would bring a crisis that would wreck New York, and bring desolation to all these splendid mansions around us. What good is property unless the title is safe? What use is this building unless the title is sure, and what is Christ to you if you cannot say: "I am sure." The devil came into the world with a doubt, and he is going down into perdition leading the crowd of the lost, with the unbeliever in the front. Doubt, then, is the damning sin of the Gospel, and the fatal broken link in every chain of human hope where it gets in. Today the most dangerous thing in the teaching of thousands—even in the ministers of the Gospel—is the element of doubt that is coming into the authority of these scriptures of truth. God wants us to believe positively. The words sceptic and agnostic simply mean one that is not sure. He will say: "All right; it may be as you say, but I don't know it is so." Now, beloved, what better are you than the infidel if you don't know. God wants you to believe your Bible without a doubt, and take the truths of Christianity, and say, "I am sure that these things are so." I dare not preach a word to you unless I believe it with my deepest soul, and have it written on the very fibres of my heart in letters of blood. God wants us to say about Christian doctrines: "I am sure." We stand in this place, by the help of God, to say: "We know whereof we speak, and believe whereof we affirm. We believe and are sure that He is the Christ, the Son of the living God, the Saviour of the world."

14

Beloved, let us be sure of what we believe. God puts His yea before His promises, and He wants us to put our amen afterwards without equivocation or ambiguity.

Then, we want to be sure not only of the truth, we want to be sure of our own salvation. We want to be sure our sins are forgiven, and God gives that right to every believer, and that word to every man who will become a believer. You may know your sins are forgiven, and if you do not, you will never have any real joy or power.

Then we need certainty in our work to know that God is in it and is going to carry it through. We must work with confidence, and must work with God's own assured presence, we must work in hope and faith. Depressed soldiers that go on the battlefield without conscious prestige, are almost sure to be beaten and prestige means a certainty of victory. So it is in the work of God.

Some of you know how much we have had to trust God in the work He is leading us to do; some of you know how, step by step, in these past years, we have gone out into enterprises that seemed impossible, and as we went on were threatened again and again with failure and defeat; and some of you know how just in that way God bade us believe and doubt not. Some of you know how, again and again, the greatest blessings of the work God gave us just after it seemed to be impossible seemed to be refused, and to be buried in disaster, and so God wants us to have that trust in His work which can say: "The God of Heaven, He will help us, therefore we, His servants, will arise and build." He has helped us, and He will never fail us. I want to speak with great carefulness and modesty today, for I wish that we might all get very low before God, and if the Lord permits us to go on with our work in this place, all our faith and power must come to us at the feet of Jesus. But I will mention this little incident: Only three days ago, when, humanly speaking, it seemed impossible that this congregation should gather here this morning in this place on account of difficulties

15

and barriers in the way, and legal points that had to be settled, there were two of God's dear children who said: "If this congregation don't worship in the Madison Avenue Tabernacle on Sunday morning, I shall be much surprised." There was no earthly ground for that, but just the confidence that God had been leading this people, and that He would still lead on. And how wondrously He has worked to fulfil their prayer and confidence, I dare not now fully tell you. I don't think God wants ever to have anything that has not got the stamp of faith upon it and the seal of God. I don't think I can have much faith in Him without trials. I have never been able to trust God much until the darkness. That trust which is easy is not faith; it is just probability.

IV.

There is one word more, and that is the word "fulness," and then I leave this benediction with you. We want not only Jesus, not only assurance, but we want the whole blessing of our Lord. Now, the world is not only full of half-believing people, but it is full of half-starved people – people that have just enough to make them hungry for more, but not enough to satisfy them; religion enough to make them miserable, and not Christ enough to make them triumphant. Balaam had just enough religion to make him lose a splendid fortune. He lost God on one side and the world on the other. They have enough principle to make them afraid to do much wrong, but they do not have much enjoyment from the Lord. I am more sorry for such Christians than for unbelievers.

The Lord wants us to start on higher ground, and if we are on higher ground, to rise still higher, until we know all the depths and heights of the fulness of Christ. First, a full Gospel. We find our Bibles are like telescopes, you see more worlds of truth as they open up more fully. By a full Gospel I mean something like this: Jesus, the

16

Son of God; Jesus, the Son of Man; Jesus crucified for sin, with real nails and real blood, and real atonement for real sin. We want that red, crimson blood from yonder cross, and not the milk and water theology of some today; real sin and real satisfaction. Again, we want a risen Christ, a Christ not risen on Easter morning only, but rising all the year round, a living Christ every day and hour. And, then, Christ coming again in His kingly glory, for that is the Gospel of the kingdom – coming to put down the disorder and the devil, and give His people righteousness and rest. That is the full Gospel.

Again, you want a full salvation as well as a full Gospel. That means, on our side, we want full pardon and no doubt about it, full life in our heart, and life giving us power and victory over temptation, and sustaining impulses for all that a life of obedience and holiness requires. And, then, it means physical life – full salvation for the body as well as the soul, and the mind – the body of Christ united to me, so that He is united to my life and keeps my body strong, as well as my soul.

I suppose there are some here this morning that have been a little prejudiced against the doctrine of Divine Healing. It is only a very small part of the full Gospel of Christ, and what we do believe about it is strangely misunderstood. A great many people believe that we claim we have power to heal men's bodies. Nobody but an imposter makes any such claim. We have no such mission. There may be something in animal magnetism, and perhaps some bodies are charged with physical life so that they can give a little of their surplus to others, but that is not what we profess. All we believe is this: That Jesus Christ is able to do all for His children that they take Him for, and all we do is to lead them to His feet, and say: "There is your need, and there is His power. If you can touch Him closely enough, you will get that need supplied, but it is all from His loving hand." We believe that the Son of Man today is a living man as much as He

17

was when He stood beside Mary in the garden. We believe He has a body like our own, bones and flesh as well as you, for we are members of His body and His flesh and His bones, and we believe that the body of Christ is for His suffering people; that He shared His bodily strength with His own disciples, even as He does spiritual strength. We have this in Him. That is what He says in John 4: "I am the living Bread; My flesh I will give for the life of the world." But this is not all of the Gospel. Jesus wants to be everything to you – power for your weakness, joy for your sorrow, peace for your distraction, control over the circumstances of life, answers to your prayers, a Master to work for, and a King to share with you by and by His everlasting throne and crown. This is full salvation for spirit, soul, and body. "I pray God that your whole spirit, soul and body be preserved blameless unto the coming of Jesus." May the Lord grant it to you all.

I can only touch these thoughts, but I want you to notice that we do not get power until we get full. Some of you know how the steam engine works. Now, suppose the boiler was just half full of steam, you could not move the train. Suppose it was nearly full, only an inch from the brim, it would not move; only does it begin to move when the boiler is full of steam. When is a Christian able to do good? When he is half full? No. When he is nine-tenths full? No; but when he is running over so full that he cannot help loving others and serving them for Christ's sake. You know how a little spring of water runs the wheel of machinery. It does not run it unless it is running over the dam. Then it gives power to the wheels; and, so, we must keep the water over the line and we shall have power. A great many people come into this Christian life just as though they moved into a house with one room in it, and they have lived in it for years. God's house is a seven-roomed house. It is not only a refuge from the storm, but it is a banquet house where they can be fed; it is a chamber of rest where they can repose on His bosom; it is a library where they can study and know His Word and will; it is an observatory where they can look out over all the landscape. I am sorry to say that I lived a long time in the kitchen. It was a long time before I got into the chamber of peace; it was a good while before I got into the workroom. I am only beginning to get into the observatory, where I can look abroad and see God's great horizons. But this morning I put in your hand the key to every part, and on that key is written "Jesus." You can go then just where you please. Come, dear friends, into this full salvation.

And, finally, God wants us to come into full work for Him. He wants His church to be complete in every department of work; He wants us to have not only the mere preaching of the Gospel, but work for the poor and lowly; work for the destitute, the sick; work for the rich and worldly. He wants us to be a people who will combine under Christ's name every department of Christian beneficence which it is right for the church of God to sustain; not to have one man preaching to a thousand men every day, but a hundred men and women working for the Lord in one blessed circle – nay, a thousand busy workers. May the Lord give us this fulness of the Gospel of Christ, this fulness of Christ Himself.

O, may He save us from disappointing Him. I remember seeing a mother once weeping over the dead body of her boy; and, as I stood there in dumb silence and heard her tell how she had loved him, borne him, sacrificed for him, served him; how she had given for him all the joy of her life, how she had trusted him to be the stay of her closing years, and how only yesterday, after a life of sin, he had broken her heart by taking his own life, after refusing for months even to speak one word to that mother; and, as she wrung her hands and told me how he had disappointed her heart and blighted her past, I think I never saw such heart-breaking grief.

O, beloved, how must God feel about us after He has given us His heart's blood, put so many advantages in our way, expended upon us so much grace and care, if we should disappoint Him. It makes my spirit cry: "Who is sufficient for these things." The Lord help us to be faithful; help us never to put Him to shame, but at last to be able to say: "Blessed Lord, I have finished the work Thou didst give me." Evermore I see before me the time when you and I shall stand on yonder shore and look back upon the years that have been, these few short years of time. O, may we cast ourselves at Jesus' feet and say: "Many a time have we faltered, many a hard fight has come, but You have kept me and held me, thanks to God who has given me the victory through the Lord Jesus Christ." From the battlefields of the Peninsula, a little band of veterans came forth, and they gave each a medal with the names of all their battles on one side, and on the other side this little sentence: "I was there." O, when that hour shall come, may it be a glad, glad, glad thought to look back on this first Sabbath of May, and the toils and sacrifices of these days, and remember: "I was there; I was there, and by the help of God and the grace of Jesus, I am here."

CHAPTER II.

CHRISTIAN LIFE
IN THE FOUR GOSPELS

"I am come that they might have life, and that they might have it more abundantly." – Jn. 10:19.

WE will look, this morning, at Christian life as it is unfolded in the four Gospels – Christ's pictures of the believers' life in these four chapters of the I New Testament: the Gospel of Matthew, Mark, Luke and John. It is an old and accepted truth that these four gospels are God's four pictures of His dear Son; that just as you cannot get any one picture of a mountain that will present all its sides, but you must look at it from many standpoints, so Christ is to be viewed from every side, and then all are to be combined to give a just comprehension of His character and completeness. They are not, therefore, four repetitions, but they are four distinct points of view of the greatest of characters. North and south, and east and west, we take our stand and we look at this mountain of divine majesty, and even then the half has not been seen.

Some of you know it was the favorite illustration of the old fathers to represent these four Gospels under the figures of the cherubim – the four symbolic forms that we find at the gate of Eden in the Hebrew Tabernacle in the visions of Ezekiel, and in the Apocalypse of St. John, namely: the lion, the ox, the man and the eagle. These four figures, you will remember, were combined in the cherubic symbol which supported the Shekinah manifestation of God in the tabernacle of Moses, a also the throne in Heaven, as John reveals it.   These four

21

figures represent the four aspects of Christ. The lion is kingly majesty; the ox is patient service; the man's face expresses His human heart, and the eagle's soaring wing His lofty and divine majesty.

So these four figures represent the four Gospels: Matthew representing Him as the King, Mark representing Him as the Servant, Luke representing Him as the Man, and John representing Him as the Son of God; Matthew's symbol being the lion. Mark's the ox, Luke's the man, and John's the soaring eagle mounting up to the heights of glory beyond man's conception or thought.

This morning, I wish to apply them differently – not to Christ, but to the Christian, for "as He is so are we also in this world;" and, if these four Gospels contain God's picture of Jesus, they surely contain God's picture of the disciples of Jesus. As the Master, so the servant; for, beholding as in a glass the glory of the Lord, we are changed into the same image, from glory to glory, even as by the spirit of the Lord. We shall then find our ideal in these four Gospels – not only in the example of Jesus, but in the teachings of Jesus in these wonderful records.

I.

First, Matthew presents to us a special ideal of Christian life and character. The one word that expresses Matthew's thought is RIGHTEOUSNESS. Matthew wrote from the Jewish standpoint, and his vision of Christ all through is that of the Jewish Christ, the Messiah that fulfils the prophecies of their Scriptures and the righteousness of their law; and, therefore, the very first teachings of Christ in the Gospel of Matthew are about righteousness. His most fundamental address is the sermon on the mount, and the one theme that runs through the whole of it is the righteousness of the kingdom. Its keynote is this: "Seek ye first the kingdom of God and His righteousness, and all these things shall be added unto you." And, again: "Except your righteousness shall exceed the righteousness of the scribes and Pharisees, you shall not enter into the kingdom of Heaven." Matthew's idea of the Christian is a line that we must stand up to and that we meet, a law that we must accept and fulfil and obey. And so this sermon goes on to say: "Not one jot or one tittle of the law shall pass away." "Whosoever shall break the least of these commandments shall be the least in the kingdom of Heaven, but whosoever shall do and teach them shall be great in the kingdom of Heaven." It is to be right, to do right, and its highest point is that sublime word: "Be ye therefore perfect even as your Father in Heaven is perfect."

It requires that we shall keep God's law not only in the outward act, but in the motives of our heart. Purity is freedom from the thought of uncleanness; love is the purpose to do no harm to your brother; murder is hating your brother; beneficence is "Let not your right hand know what your left hand doeth." It is singleness of motive. "Let thine eye be single and thy whole body shall be full of light." "No man can serve two masters." And from this comes trust in God, because if you have but one motive and one aim, you will be able to trust implicitly, and without singleness of purpose you cannot have trust. That is Matthew's picture of a righteous man – a man who not only outwardly, but in his deepest soul, chooses the will of God and seeks to fulfil it literally and truly, and never rests satisfied with anything less than the will and the glory of his Father which is in Heaven.

That is Christ's first public address in Matthew, and how you and I are ever going to lower the standard of Christian life in the face of that, I cannot tell. How it is possible that the church of God has got down to its miserable level, I don't know. There stands that great rock elevation for centuries; Jesus has never made a lower platform for you and me. What are we going to do, then? How are we going to live that kind of righteousness? Jesus has given us a golden ladder that leads us up, and we have it in the seven or eight beatitudes: "Blessed are the poor in spirit, for theirs is the kingdom of Heaven; blessed are they that mourn, for they shall be comforted; blessed are the meek, for they shall inherit the earth; blessed are they that hunger and thirst after righteousness, for they shall be filled; blessed are the merciful, for they shall obtain mercy; blessed are the poor in heart, for they shall see God; blessed are the messengers of peace, for they shall be called the children of God." That is the ladder. I think if you will look at it carefully, you will see in it a wonderful stair. The very first rung in it is absolute despair of ever attaining to that righteousness yourself. The very first step you have to take is to give it up yourself, and say: "Lord, I have not got that righteousness at all; I am destitute of all." That is to be poor in spirit. That is the way to get righteousness, and so the very first word in this scale of righteousness is unrighteousness, the lack of righteousness. It is a step down. I want to climb to that glorious mount of God, and I go downward first – away down to nothing, "Poor in spirit" – and the moment we get there, "Theirs is the kingdom of Heaven."

I have got it all now, because 1 haven't got anything; because I have got down to the place where I give up my attempts, and now God is going to come and give me His righteousness; my righteousness has failed, but I see it. There was the failure of the scribes and Pharisees. They would not see their failure; they would not take that first step down; they would not recognize their unrighteousness; "and going about to establish their own righteousness, they would not submit themselves to the righteousness of God, for Christ is the end of the law for righteousness to every one that believeth." He comes with righteousness for the unrighteous, and when you see

24

your unrighteousness, then He comes in with His divine perfection. Beloved, we teach no human perfection. There is no human perfection in any, but there is perfection in God, and He will put His perfect spirit in your heart and be your righteousness if you let Him.

So the very first step to this righteousness of Matthew is poor in spirit. Then the next is a little deeper: "They that mourn." Because now you must get plastic, you must get broken, you must get like the metal in the fire, which the Master can mold; and so, it is not enough to see your unrighteousness, but deeply to feel it, deeply to regret it, deeply to mourn over it, to count it not a little thing that sin has come into your life. And so God leads a soul unto His own righteousness. He usually leads it through some testings and trials. This generally comes after conversion. I do not think it necessary for a soul to have deep and great suffering before it is saved. I think He will put it into the fire when it knows it is saved; when it realizes it is accepted; when it is not afraid of the discipline; when it is not the hand of wrath, but the hand of love. O, then God takes you down and makes you poor in spirit, and makes you mourn until you get to the third step, which is to be meek, broken, yielded, submissive, willing, surrendered and laid low at His feet, crying: "What wilt Thou have me to do?" No dogmatic pride, no standing out and saying: "I will not have it this way; I must have it that way;" but, "Lord, save me from this body of death; give me Thy righteousness at any cost."

And then, the fourth step: They that hunger and thirst after righteousness. O, what a hunger you get now to be pure. You have seen your impurity, you have seen your mighty lack, and now you long to be like God, to have His heart in your heart and His nature in your soul; and, when all this has come, you are ready for His righteousness. Then Christ puts into you His mercifulness and purity of heart, and sends you with His

25

messages of peace to bring men into union with God – "peace-makers," messengers of the Gospel; and then, when He has got all those things done, He puts you into the fire once more to harden the impressions, to make fast the picture, so that the last view is "They that are persecuted for righteousness' sake, for theirs is the kingdom of Heaven." This is God's righteousness. It is to see, O beloved, that God does want from you and me a very high standard of right; that He will take no less from any man that He has redeemed; and then, next, to see that you have not got that, and cannot have it yourself and cannot make it out of your own materials; and then to get low down at His feet, and say: "Lord, give me Thy righteousness. Jesus Christ come into my heart and be my righteousness. I am hungry and thirsty." I am not going to put it off, and say: "It is no use trying, nobody can be perfect;" but I am going to say: "God is perfect, and God is willing to be my righteousness, and I will take no less."

Ah, that is what He wants; and then shall He fulfil to you that old promise: "This is the name wherewith He shall be called the Lord our Righteousness." And then, more wonderful still: "This is the name wherewith she shall be called – poor, sinful, Jerusalem – the Lord our Righteousness. He is perfect righteousness – you the same in Him, because He becomes your righteousness. You take your husband's name, wear his beautiful garments and jewels, and be even as he is in this world. That is Matthew's picture of Christian life.

Now, beloved, do you know the mistake some of you are making? Some of you say: "It is not possible for me to be good; no man ever was perfect, and it is no use for me to try." That is the mistake many of you are making. I agree with the first sentence, "No man ever was perfect," but I don't agree with the second, "There is no use trying." There is a divine righteousness that we may have. I don't mean merely that which pardons your sin –

I believe that, too – but I mean far more; I mean that which comes into your soul and unites itself with the fibers of your being; I mean Christ, your life, your purity, making you feel as Christ feels, think as Christ thinks, love as Christ loves, hate as Christ hates, and be "partakers of the divine nature." That is God's righteousness: "That the righteousness of the Lord might be fulfilled *in* us" – not by us, but IN us; nor our hands and feet merely, but our very instincts, our very desires, our very nature springing up in harmony with His own. Have you got it, dear friends? Is it all right? That is what righteousness means – to be right. Is it right here in the heart? Is it right according to your own standard and sense of right? Is it right with others? Is it right with Him? That is all the righting up we need. The world is all upside down; you are upside down, and when you get right, everything will get right also. Did you ever notice that when you are depressed everything is blue, and that when everything has become a great joy in your heart, you say: "This is the most beautiful day I ever saw." It is not any more beautiful than yesterday. O, when you get the right spirit, everything will be all right. Christ came to make things right. Is there anything wrong today, beloved? Take God's great word, and let Christ be your righteousness.

II.

Now, I come to the second picture of Christian life. It is in the Gospel of Mark, and the thought there is service. Mark is so different from Matthew, that the most superficial observer catches the spirit at a glance. It always reminds me of three or four distinguished characters of history, as I read the stirring and bracing sentences, so short that they are hardly long enough to make a complete sentence, and rushing on so rapidly that it seems like a panorama. I think of such men as Oliver

27

Cromwell or William the Silent (a man of few words but tremendous blows), or such a man as Stonewall Jackson – or such a man as General Grant, a man of very strong elements of force, yet not of many words. So Mark just dashes on, and before you have read seven verses, you are half way through the life of Christ – more than half way through. The first two or three sentences carry you on to the thirtieth year of His life, and in a few more sentences you are in the midst of His Galilean ministry. He carries yon right along with the rush of work until, before you know it, it is all over, and you see Him ascending to His throne. And lo, He is working still for the very last sentence in Mark is: "The Lord working with them and confirming the Word with sings following." Mark is not a talker, but a worker. It is busy, intense activity all through. And the words spoken in Mark to us about Christian life are all about work. It is the picture of Christ at work, like the ox toiling at the plow, and then lying down on the altar to die. It is the picture of our work, too. As Mr. Spurgeon says, "it sets us all on the go;" for it is go all the way through. We read the first miracle, and it is: "Go show thyself to the priests." And then we read another, and it is: "Go home to thy friends and tell them what the Lord hath done for thee, and how He hath had compassion." And we read a little further on, and it is: "Go and tell Peter and His disciples that He has risen from the dead." And then, a little further it is: "Go into all the world and preach the gospel to every creature." It is "go" all the way through; and if you are going to keep up with Mark, you have to go very fast and you have to keep going, and you have to go with the Master with you and in you as your spirit and power for service.

Now, a mere cold righteousness is not enough. We want a practical Christianity. Matthew won't do without Mark. Matthew without Mark would be a splendid statue up there in the gallery, but when you put Mark in it is a ministering angel of love and service. Some people are very well to look at when you do not break the crust, but when you put them into the busy test of life, they do not stand. They are beautiful Christians in the prayer meeting, but put them down town, or send them up five or six stories to an attic, and they break down. They have not got the "go" in them. They do not do enough. They will talk about what they are going to do, but when the time comes they do not do it. It is talk, not work; but Mark goes just ahead, and when he gets through you begin to talk about the work that he did, but he does not say a word about himself. There is not one long address in Mark. There is only one little parable, and it is all about work. It is all busy energy, and it tells us of a Christian life that does something for Christ, and is all the time doing in His glorious strength. There is a word in Mark that many of you have marked a great deal. It is the word "straightway." "Straightway He went with them." "Straightway they left all and followed Him." "Immediately he was made whole."

There is no losing of time. It is all prompt, vigorous, energetic and right in the nick of time. The work of Mark is full of self-denial. "Rising up in the morning a great while before day." People thronged upon Him, full of tender compassion, full of prayerful dependence upon God. "He retired into the wilderness and prayed." It is full of wide, aggressive work for the world.

I cannot dwell, however, on the picture. It is enough to sketch it. This is the second element in spiritual Christianity. It is aggressive, it is active, it is vigorous, it does something, and it goes on doing to the glorious end, and is nothing more or less than Christ in your working. I tell you, dear friends, if you get Christ in your heart you will not want to lie on the lounge and dream, but you will be glad to live for souls and work for God until the end comes; and the nearer you get to the Master, the more will you want to save the lost.

III.

Third, let us look at Luke's picture. Now, Luke is the picture of another element of Christian life which is even more important than the other two. Matthew is righteousness, Mark is service, Luke is love. Its symbol is the face of a man. It is the human heart. It is the human smile. It is the human tenderness and the divine love blending all. You know Luke was the large-hearted Gentile, representing broader elements than any of the other disciples or evangelists, and therefore a better type of large-hearted humanity than any of them. So his gospel just teems with this sweet spirit of humanness and of love. The first picture we get of human love in Luke is the woman weeping at His feet. That is love starting out. "She loved much." The next picture in the eighth chapter is Mary Magdalene, out of whom He had cast seven spirits, loving, following Jesus, ministering to Him, giving up her home, giving up her money, and being consecrated for service.

Then, again, the next is the picture of the Good Samaritan in Luke – the man that found the poor traveler beaten and bruised, took him on his own beast to an inn, paid his fair and then left enough to provide for him – love to the suffering. The next is: "Go out into the hedges and highways; constrain them to come in that My house may be filled." There is love seeking the lost as well as seeking the suffering, and "constraining them to come in." That is not much like some of our congregations today; not much like the best of them today; not much like us today, or we would have every second pew filled with people that would keep a good many fashionable Christians away. We have not done enough of it yet. We have not wanted to do enough of it yet. I do not want to keep anybody away. We want fashion to melt away in the love of the lost. We want it to go itself and bring in both the poor and the rich; but

30

we have not enough of the love that constrains so that they can't help coming.

Then, the next is still deeper. The prodigal son, the good shepherd, the woman sweeping the house for her coin – the love of the shepherd, and the woman and the father reproduced in us for souls. And so I might go on and speak of the conversion of Zacheus, and the love that saved him; of Jesus weeping over Jerusalem, of his love for the dying thief, and many other instances of the same holy tenderness.

Now, put these three together and you have the three sides of what God expects you to be: Righteousness, through God's own righteousness; practical service; and love that makes you tender, gentle, human, approachable, winning, constraining, weeping at the feet of Jesus, weeping over Jerusalem, and seeking until you find the prodigal and the wandering sheep, and the soul more precious than coin of silver or gold. That is love. If we get these three sides in our Christian life, we shall be well-nigh complete.

Now, dear friends, just pause a moment before we pass from this third picture, and ask the Lord for what Tennyson speaks of in one of his poems:

"Ask Heaven for a human heart."

And you will never get a human heart until it is born from above, from the heart of Christ. For man has lost his holy humanity and too often has got a demon heart. God wants us, as Christians, to be simple, human, approachable and childlike. The Christians that I know and love best, and that are nearest to the Lord, are the most simple. Whenever we grow stilted we are only fit for a picture gallery, and we are only good on a pedestal; but, if we are going to live among men, and love and save them, we must be approachable and human. All the stiffness is but another form of self-consciousness. Ask

31

Christ for a human heart, for a smile that will be as easy as your own little one in your presence. O, how much Christ did by little touches. He never would have got at the woman of Samaria if he had come to her as the prophet. He sat down a tired man, and said: "Give Me a drink of water." And so, all through His life, it was His simple humanness and love that led Him to others, and led them to Him and to His great salvation.

IV.

Fourth. Now, finally, I come to the last chapter of Christian life in the gospel of John, and that b rings me to my text; "I am come that they might have life, and that they might have it more abundantly." Matthew is righteousness, Mark is service, Luke is love, but John is LIFE – without which there can be no righteousness, without which there can be no real, living service, without which there can be no divine love in the dead, cold heart. John brings us in the life – nay, the springing, boundless life – life more abundantly. This thought would be theme enough for a whole morning. I can, therefore, only send you to your Bibles, as I send you home, to trace this divine thought of life in John.

First, the life comes in from Heaven through Jesus Himself. "In Him was life." – John 1:4. There was the beginning of life. It had died out from us, and so it had to come back with Him. "In Him was life, and the life was the light of men." He came down the Eternal Life of God, and they got life by getting Him. "This is the record that God hath given to us – eternal life, and this is life in His Son. He that hath the Son hath life; he that hath not the Son of God hath not life." He is the true Son of God, and he is eternal life. Jesus is eternal life. Eternal life is not a thing. Eternal life is Jesus Christ, and you will never get it until you get His loving heart within you. "This is the true God and eternal life." That was

32

the last word that John said about Christ in his great epistle. It is not an *it;* it is not some thing; it is HIM living in your heart and making everything alive.

Dear friends, this Christian life is a stupendous miracle. It is nothing more nor less than an eternal God personally living in the heart. O, if you could see it you would bow down in awe before the majesty of such a presence, even in the humblest believer by your side, for that is the temple of the living God. O, if Moses took off his shoes from off his feet when he saw God in a burning bush, surely we might well prostrate ourselves with awe when we see God in a living, human soul, personally dwelling there; and, if you just realized that it is true of you, you would go through life with the very dignity and majesty of the Son of God; you would not dare to do anything mean; you would walk with the steps of a king, because you bear in your bosom the jewel of the presence and majesty of Jehovah, the great I AM.

Now, trace this a little further. In the third chapter of John, we see this life new-born: "Except a man be born again, he cannot see the kingdom of God." "Born," therefore you have got life. Christ is born in you just the same as He was born in Bethlehem. Again, you go into the fourth chapter. We see this life dwelling in the heart as a fountain of life. "If thou knewest the gift of God, and who it is that said, Give me a drink! Thou wouldst have asked him and given him the living water. He that drinketh of this water shall thirst again, but he that drinketh of the water that I shall give him, shall never thirst; the water that I shall give him shall be in him a well of water springing up into everlasting life." That is a well in your heart springing up and overflowing.

You know that some people are always wanting to go to some meeting or other to get life; but if you have the well in your heart, you do not need to go anywhere else. You have got the throne, and the King and the Answerer of prayer here. This is Heaven, and there you abide in

His presence. Have you got that, dear friends? That is life indeed springing up to everlasting life beyond.

We go on to the fifth chapter of John, and we see this eternal life, twenty-fourth verse: "Verily, verily, I say unto you, he that heareth My word and believeth on him that sent Me hath everlasting life, and shall not come into condemnation, but is passed from death unto life." it runs on beyond this period of existence. It is everlasting life, and he that has it shall never come into condemnation. In the sixth chapter, there is life for the body as well as the soul. "He that eateth My flesh and drinketh My blood hath eternal life, and dwelleth in Me and I in him." "My flesh is meat indeed, and My blood is drink. He that eateth Me, even he shall live by Me." If you have got this life, it will be the very body and flesh of the Son of God nourishing your brain, your heart and your whole physical being.

Again, we go on in the seventh chapter of John, and we have got a higher life still: "He that believeth on Me, as the Scripture hath said, out of his belly shall flow rivers of living water." That is the life overflowing. It is a well above the brim, and the water is running out like rivers of blessing to the world around you, so that now you cannot retain it. Now, you serve and help others without trying. It is spontaneous and irrepressible, and a delight to you to bless. And now it is rivers. It is large, now. When you were only enjoying it yourself, it was a well; but when you are giving it to the word, it is a river. That is what makes it easy to serve. You cannot help it. You would be miserable any other way. When Christ's life fills your heart it must have vent.

John Bunyan went to his prison home and sat down there on the stone floor, and wrote: "So they had me home to prison, and I sat down and wrote, and I wrote because joy did make me write." That was John Bunyan's service. It was rivers of living water running over. Prison home! A little stone his desk, and the
34

angels his companions; and millions today reading the book that is the most widely circulated on earth except the Bible and one other little book – the greatest book of the age after God's, because it was a river from a fountain. There is no work goes far unless it comes for the depths. O, that is what you want, beloved. You want a work that runs over. Then the work is easy.

We might trace the life still further in John, and find that it is resurrection life; that it is life not of nature – not the old natural life – but it is the life that comes after death. I mean after the death of self, after the death of sin; for he says still later on: "I am the resurrection and the life. He that believeth in Me, though he were dead, yet shall he live." "Except a corn of wheat fall into the ground and die it abideth alone, but if it die it bringeth forth much fruit." "He that loveth his life shall love it, but he that hateth his life in this world shall keep it unto life eternal."

That is the highest thing in life. It is the life that gave up its own self-will, that dies to its own desire, and that rose with the risen Christ to a higher and a grander life, to die no more. So that before you can have much life, beloved, you must die to something; you must die to everything that is not in harmony with Christ's life. There must be a Good Friday before there can be an Easter; there must be the taking down before there can be the going up; there must be the going out before there can be the coming in.

Dear friends, are you willing to have these four pictures – this righteousness, this service, this love and this life? If you are, He has it for you; and all you need is to get your self out and let Him come in, and when He lives you shall live also. It is a very simple thing when the heart is right. It is not climbing up with your own efforts, but it is coming down and taking Christ as your glorious life. O, how easy spring is, and yet how hard it is to make spring in winter. Go into one of those Fifth

35

avenue green houses, and see them in the month of January trying to make spring. What an effort. How they have to bring in the artificial heat and force the poor plants beyond their natural tendencies and instincts, and then after all it is a poor place – a few flowers and a sickly sort of heat, constant labor and care and an enormous expense. But wait until the month of April or May, and look at yonder arbor, or go into the wild fields of nature, and see what the Great Gardener can do without an effort; see how little pruning is necessary; no need to take away the old leaves, but the springing life of nature throws them off, and she covers herself with robes of glory which Solomon never wore. So easy, so simple – easy because there is life there. In the other case it is an effort. So a great many people are trying to raise God's fruits and flowers in the green house. O, take them out into the spring, get the divine life upon them and within them, and it will be so easy, so free, so full, and so abounding with the fullness of the blessing of Christ. May the Lord show us His ideal and our helplessness, and then may He show us Himself and find a welcome in your heart as your everlasting life, as your divine righteousness, as your boundless power and as your living love for Jesus' sake, Amen.

CHAPTER III.

CHRISTIAN LIFE IN ACTS
LIFE IN THE SPIRIT

"But ye shall receive power after that the Holy Ghost is come upon you; and ye shall be witnesses unto Me both in Jerusalem, and in all Judea, and in Samaria, and to the uttermost part of the earth." – Acts 1:8.

"And with great power gave the Apostles witness of the resurrection of the Lord Jesus; and great grace was upon them all." – Acts 4:33.

---

*L*AST Sabbath morning, I spoke to you about Christian life as revealed to us in the Gospels of Matthew, Mark, Luke and John. This morning, I want to go with you through the Book of Acts, the early annals of Christianity, the story of primitive piety, and learn some lessons for our nineteenth century from the first, with respect to the true spirit of Christian life. The words that I have read present a sort of table of contents of the Book of Acts, and they are amplified in the subsequent chapters.

This wonderful book might be called a fifth Gospel. It contains the story of Jesus Christ in continuance, commencing where Jesus left off, and revealing to us the ascended Lord Jesus as they revealed the incarnate Jesus Christ; so that another name for it would happily and properly be the Gospel of the risen Christ – of the reigning Lord. Dwelling, however, not so especially this morning on the general features of the book as upon the forms of Christian character it reveals, let us glance first at the most important of them, namely: that Christian life in the Acts of the Apostles is always connected with the personal indwelling of the Holy Ghost. "Ye shall receive power after that the Holy Ghost has come upon you." Another personality now stands before our view – no longer the second person Jesus, but one Just as distinct and personal, just as mighty and glorious, but called by another name – the Holy Ghost. Before Christ left them He gave them notice of this: "The Comforter will come to you. I will send Him from the Father. It is expedient that I go, for if I go not away, He cannot come to you." So it is a distinct person in every sense of the word, a substitute for Christ, one who came and took Christ's ministry as He had left it, and has been carrying it on ever since; not an influence or an atmosphere, not a radiation of divine love and life, but a living, concrete person, as real as you and I, as any angel in Heaven, as any substance in the universe who has come to take the place of Christ in the world, and has been residing here for eighteen centuries – not residing in Heaven now (for the Holy Ghost is not in Heaven as His home), but residing on earth ever since the day of Pentecost, just as Jesus resided on earth for thirty-three years before; residing in your heart as really as your beating heart is there, as really as your immortal spirit is there, so there is one besides that – the Holy Ghost.

The Holy Spirit of God as a living person, is the beginning, and the middle and the consummation of all the apostolic life. They cannot do a thing apart from Him. They have to wait ten days in silence until He comes, doing nothing but praying and waiting for His descent. Even the premature suggestion of Peter about Matthias came to nought, and the new apostle was quietly ignored by the Lord. There was nothing for them to do until the Holy Spirit came, and then after He came there was nothing they could do that was worth doing without His influence, presence, guidance and power. Henceforth we see this Spirit the spring of everything in their life. They become absolutely transformed. Men that shrank before from the threat of a girl, stand undaunted before the throne of the Cæsars and all the authority of Herod or the Jews. Why? Because they had received into them another mind, another nature, another person – the Holy Spirit of the eternal and Almighty God. And so their preaching became mighty and effectual. They never attributed it to their own eloquence, but His enduement. They could not become even useful deacons without Him. They called men full of the Holy Ghost and wisdom to administer the finances of the church.

The Apostolic Church never thought of appointing a man to any sacred office without the Holy Ghost. The greatest amount of common sense was no qualification; the very largest bank balance that he could have to make up deficiencies would not answer; he must be a man full of the Holy Ghost and wisdom, or he could not even be a deacon in the church of God.

Then, again, in all their work it was the Holy Ghost who guided their movements. He said: "Separate me Barnabas and Saul for the work to which I have called them." The Holy Ghost sent them both to their mission field, and as they went forth through their field they would have preached here and there, but the Holy Ghost suffered them not. "They were forbidden by the Spirit to preach in Asia." Thus they went, ever dependent on the Holy Ghost. When they are filled with sorrow and suffering, it is the Holy Ghost that comforts them. "Then were the disciples filled with joy and with the Holy Ghost." Paul finds certain people at Ephesus and he says: "Have you received the Holy Ghost since you believed?" And they say: "We have not so much as heard whether there be any Holy Ghost." And then he told them they must make a new start, and receive the Spirit of God and be baptized for their work.

O, friends, have you received the Holy Ghost since you believed? This is the secret of effectual Christian life, and the only source of power in ministering for God. I do not mean, have you been converted. I do not mean, have you been a real, an honest, a constant church member – for all that is possible – but have you gone further? Have you offered yourself entirely to be possessed by the indwelling God? That is a great deal more. It is one thing for the Spirit of God to touch you and put a spiritual life in you and pass on, and then visit you occasionally on Sabbath days and at communion services, and when you bow down to pray, but it is another thing for Him to come and reside within you continually, the Lord of every motion, the Giver of every thought, the Power of every act; and I dare not say that every Christian has this Holy Ghost personally welcomed and dominant in his heart. I dare not say that I had for many years of my Christian life – I dare not say that I was not a Christian man years before I knew this, and that I preached the Gospel at least ten years before I knew what it was to have a personal, divine presence living and manifesting His reality in my brain, my affections, my will, my body, my thought, my work – the indwelling Holy Spirit: and I am sure He never came to me in that way, as the occupant of my house, until I gave Him the house and became no longer the owner of the house, but a lodger in it, and He the proprietor taking care of me and using me.

Dear friends, if you come to this place, that is the Christianity of the Acts of the Apostles. At its threshold there stands the divine presence, knocking at your door, saying: "Will you let Me in? Hitherto I have given you much. I have led you to Jesus, I have given you pardon, but now may I come in and dwell; may I come in and rule; may I come in and live there, and be the impulse and the power of your life?"

Up to this time you know Peter was saved, and John was saved, and James was saved, and Andrew was saved. They were all saved, but they did not have the power of

40

the Holy Ghost: and what were they worth when the trial of the cross came, when even the threat of the servant maid frightened the boldest of them away? And what does your religion amount to until you have the Holy Ghost; until you have this controlling, residing power carrying on all your work? This alone can sanctify your soul; this alone can comfort you under all circumstances; this alone can be a spring of joy that is not dependent on outward success and prosperity. This alone can make your words go to the hearts and consciences of men. This alone can make your prayers cleave through these spaces and reach the throne of God, and set in motion the machinery of Providence and power. This alone can make you a living force in the world like God himself. Have you received the Holy Ghost? God says, "The Holy Ghost whom He hath given to all that they obey Him." That is the trouble – that is the secret. Are you willing from this hour to obey Him under all circumstances, regardless of consequences? Are you willing to surrender yourselves to be used for Him – not merely to get a great and mighty engine that can run your trains, but to let the Engineer himself direct it, and to let it run on His rails and His tracks, and carry His burdens? You can have Him, you can have God, but you cannot have God to use Him for your unworthy or selfish purposes. If you are willing to obey Him, you can enter on all the possibilities of the Acts of the Apostles. If you do not, you are away back there where Peter was – in the uncertainty, the doubt, the inconstancy and the peril of many a denial and many a failure, and many a terrible fall. Here in this place, this morning, God speaks to you. Have you received the Holy Ghost since you believed? Are you willing today to offer yourself up for His indwelling? Do you realize what a majestic existence you will have? Do you recognize what a sacredness it will give to your life? Do you recognize what an awe will hover over you, and yet what a holy gladness, saying to yourself: "Knowest thou not that thou art the temple of the Living God, for He hath said, 'I will dwell in them and I will walk in them.'" May the Lord enable you to take His Holy Spirit. O, how willing He is to come.

> "A gracious, willing guest,
> Where He can find one humble heart
> Wherein to rest."

O, let the open door welcome Him in; until you do, it is a poor, lost battle. "The Spirit lusteth against the flesh, and the flesh lusteth against the Spirit." That is not your spirit, but it is God's Spirit. The Holy Spirit lusteth against the flesh. It is Spirit with capital S. I did – I am sorry to say that I did – for a long time try with my spirit to fight the flesh, but it was no use. But I found one day that it was all in the kind of letter I spelled it with; but when I let the Holy Spirit, I found that He could fight the battle I could not."

"I will put My Spirit within you, and I will cause you to walk in My statutes, and ye shall keep My judgments." "I will put My fear in your hearts, and ye shall not turn away from Me." O, friends, would not that be blessed, would not that be such a rest for you, all worn out with this strife in your own strength? Do you not want a strong man to conquer the strong man of self and sin? Do you not want a leader? Do you not want God himself to be with you, to be your occupant? Do you not want rest? Are you not conscious of this need? O, this sense of being beaten back, longing, wanting, but not accomplishing. That is what he comes to do. "Ye shall receive power after the Holy Ghost has come upon you." Better than that: "Ye shall receive the power of the Holy Ghost coming upon you." That is the true version, and really it is immensely different from the other. You shall not receive power yourself, so that people shall say: "How much power he has got." You shall not have and power whatever, but you shall receive the power of the

42

Holy Ghost coming upon you, he having the power, that is all. You do not get anything yourself, but you get a presence which comes and does what you cannot do, and all the time you are depending upon Him, so that you are just as weak as ever yourself, but you have got Him to fall back upon. He is the Comforter, the Advocate, the Paraclete. The Greek word is "Paraclete," and the English word is Comforter, and the Latin Advocate. Para-klete is one I call on, or one I call to me. Advocate, one I call to me. That is, one you can call on at a moment's notice and find ready, ever on hand at His post, night or day in peril or safety. O, it is marvelous how constant, how near at hand, is this gracious Friend. You can call upon Him in prosperity, but O, when the peril comes, when the swift tornado sweeps over the sea, when the mountains seem to be hurled from their moorings and the waves rage with satanic fury, have you never been conscious of the marvelous calm which seems to say: "It is I, be not afraid?" He is always there. Have you never awakened out of sleep with a start, and just for a moment seemed to forget yourself, and then in the next moment breathed the name of Jesus, and lo, He was by your side, the One ever near and ready for any emergency?

Now, that is the first feature of Apostolic Christianity. The Scriptural picture of a useful man is a man Holy Ghost and of faith. May God make you and me just such men. I would rather have ten men in my church full of the Holy Ghost than one hundred millionaires – one hundred professors of all the sciences and all the doctors of theology.

II.

Again, apostolic Christianity was marked by a second feature, namely: power. First, the Holy Ghost; secondly power. "Ye shall receive power after the Holy Ghost is come upon you." This was the age of power. This, more

43

than any other, was the age when natural power had reached its climax. Power of mind never had been so great. Just about this time was the Augustan age of Roman literature. Just a little before this had been the highest stage of Grecian art. All that the minds of men could say and write in architecture, literature or art had been done. The world never has risen any higher in natural vigor than in those days, and the greatest men of today are ready to admit it by making the classic language the basic language the basis of modern culture, by making the Grecian forms of art the unrivaled models of modern art, so that in literature and art they recognize it as the day of the world's highest power

Then, again, politically it was the age of power Daniel represented it as a beast with teeth of iron, and heels that crushed out everything, the colossal power that had defied the world and put its feet on the neck of all people. Its arms were invincible, its phalanxes were irresistible, and the idea of force was embodied in every form of Roman speech. The word man was synonymous with the word courage, signifying a man that had power in him; so that force and power were the ideal in Roman thought. Intellectual and physical power had reached their very highest point, and it needed something real to cope with these forces of thought and these forms of force. It was no child's play to stand before the Jews, and before the philosophers of Athens, and before the throne of Cæsar, and say: "I am not ashamed of the Gospel of Christ, for it is the power of God unto salvation." And Paul was not ashamed of it. And before that sword, and that arm and that Gospel, Grecian philosophy melted away, and Roman power was shattered in the dust; and, before long, the greatest of the later emperors of Rome placed the signal of the cross on his banner, and said: "In this sign I conquer." And in this age of power the Gospel was given to the world. It was a real force; and Peter, standing before that Sanhedrim, with his few, simple

44

words was able to wield a mightier force. Paul, standing before Felix and Agrippa, had a power behind him greater than Rome. Stephen, standing first before the council, and then on that field of martyrdom, was the real master. They themselves were conscious of his strange power. They could not resist the wisdom and the power with which he spoke, and in impotent fury they could only gnash upon him with their teeth and beat his life out with stones, because his love was stronger than their hatred. In half a century the world was filled with the Gospel of Jesus Christ. With no railroads to carry people over the globe, no telegraph wires to help tell the story, no newspapers to spread the tidings, but the slow, cumbrous processes of ancient travel and communications, yet in fifty years there was not an important center in the whole globe that was not reached with the Gospel of Jesus Christ. We have no such power even in our nineteenth century, though we are beginning to advance a little towards it.

And, then, in the individual life there was power. They felt these men were living forces themselves. Paul was a concentration of tremendous power, touching all the Gentile world. They were men that conquered themselves. They were men that conquered sin and temptation in their own lives. They had the same passions as we; they had the same evil, proud hearts as we; they shed the same blood on the battlefield of the heart as we shed, but they were not afraid of it, and they conquered; and because they conquered sin and self, in the name of Jesus they had power to conquer Satan. That is what the church of God is dying of today – impotency, weakness. O, when I tell you – as I have told you before – that whole churches work for years, and then there are not quite two souls added to their membership per annum and perhaps a great many backsliders; Christianity and all its machinery giving us the sad record of an average of less than two additions every year in proportion to

45

every minister of the Gospel; a choir costing a great expense – two or three thousand dollars, and a pastor costing ten or fifteen thousand, and a church costing ten or fifteen thousand, and then at the end of the year two souls counted up! Is that power? Is it not an awful shame? You don't expect results. You say: "I do what others have done, and we will just have to be content with the same while we live." Down in your heart you feel that it is a mockery and a shame; you feel that if religion is anything it is everything; you feel that if God is able to bridge over the abyss of hell, He is able to conquer sin here; if He is able to save your poor, shivering spirit in the hour of death and judgment, He is able to save it now. If you have not power enough to conquer self and sin, how shall you conquer the coming of the least enemy? O, you are not content. There is a living power you need to make actual the things you often dream about, to make demonstrable the things you only theoretically believe. You want it, dear friends. I do not believe there is a man or woman here this morning that is quite satisfied that their Christian life should be a failure. If it is, it will be a sad disappointment to you when you gather up its fragments of failure in eternity, and bring them to your Master's feet.

There is power for us if we have the Holy Ghost. God wants us to speak to men so that they will feel it so that they will never forget it. God means every Christian to be effective, to count in the actual records and results of Christian work. Dear friends, God sent you here to be a power yourself. There is not one of you but is an essential wheel of the machinery, and can accomplish all that God calls you to. I solemnly believe that there is not a thing that God expects of man but that Cod will give the man power to do. There is not a claim God makes on you or me but God will stand up to do, and will give what He commands. I believe when Christ Jesus lived and died and sent down the Holy Ghost, He sent

46

resources for all our need, and that there is no place for failure in Christian life if we will take God's resources. Jesus the ascended One, and the Holy Ghost, the indwelling energy, life and efficiency of God, are sufficient for all possible emergencies. Do you believe this? Then, let us rise to our place of power. It is not mere intellectual power – it is not social and persuasive power – it is not the power of strong character. It is the power of men and women that make others feel that God is working in them and speaking through them.

III.

The third feature of primitive Christianity is witnessing for Christ. I have dwelt chiefly on these first two thoughts because they are the basis of all else. Now, let us build up the superstructure, and then crown it. "Ye shall be witnesses unto Me." Your great business is to hold up Christ to men; to let men see not so much your life, but Christ through your life. They were witnesses to a Christ that was crucified, to a Christ that was divine, to a Christ that was risen, to a Christ that was reigning, to a Christ that was coming again. Have you noticed the sermon of Peter on the day of Pentecost, the sermons of Peter to the council, the sermon of Paul before Agrippa? Everywhere it is the story of Jesus Christ. It is nothing less. I have read these apostolic sermons again and again, and there is nothing but Christ. I used to say: "Is it with those few simple words you have such power; I have seen no eloquence in them – no pathos in them." They never spoke but it is the whole story of Jesus, and they stopped when they got through; and I tell you God used it marvelously, and I believe if we so exalt Him, the Holy Ghost will use us. We have got to hold up Christ as witnesses. Now, you know a witness in court will not be listened to if it is hearsay; a witness in court is not allowed to state anything but what he himself knows; and you will find, when you know Christ, then your witness to Christ will tell.

I am always ashamed to say it, but it is true that in the years that I did not know Christ as an indwelling Spirit in my heart, I never had a single Christian come to speak to me about their spiritual life. I was a pastor for ten years before this, and in all these ten years I seldom had a Christian come to me and say: "Dear pastor, I want you to tell me how to enter into a deeper Christian life." I had sinners come because I knew something about that and preached to sinners. But the very moment that God came into my heart and gave me this Indwelling Christ, they began to come to me; and from that time, for years, hundreds have come to be helped to find the Lord as a personal and indwelling life and power. It so touched me because I felt I had not known anything about it before, and my witness was not worth anything; but the moment I knew it personally, then they felt it and they came to find it. Dear friends, if you have got Christ in your heart, men will know it. I tell you, men know your measure spiritually. They know if this thing is a sort of bashful attempt to do your duty or if it is a spring that you cannot keep back. People who know Christ can tell of Him in a way that will make others know. You must have life to impart it; you must have fire to kindle fire; you must know Jesus to lead others to Him. People ask what I have. "I have not anything." "Well, but have not you had a great change come over you?" "I have nothing." "Well, what is it?" "It is not anything but Jesus Christ." "Well, that is very simple." Why, of course, it is very simple; every great thing is very simple. It is not I at all, it is just that Jesus Christ has become real and is real every moment. When I say that to people, they say: "Why, I thought you were something, and I became discouraged wondering if I could ever be the same." "Well, then, I am not anything." "Then, if it is only Jesus, why cannot I have Him as well as you?" "Of course you can." Dear friends, it is just linking on with another person; and, commencing this moment. You can from today go out of this place with the same relationship to Jesus Christ as anybody else has. You can take Him from this hour as the personal omnipotence of your life. That is all it is. Witness unto Him. O, praise the Lord, we may hold up a living Christ, to tell the world He is able, He is willing, He is yours. He is yours for all, forever.

IV.

Again, another feature of apostolic Christianity was aggressive work. "And ye shall be witnesses unto Me both in Jerusalem and in Judea, and in Samaria, and unto the uttermost part of the earth." Having got the Spirit and the power, and having Jesus Christ as the theme of their testimony, they went out to spread it over the world. If it was good for Peter it was good for the twelve; if it was good for twelve it was good for twenty-four; if it was good for all the disciples it was good for all Jerusalem, it was good for Judea and then for Samaria and then that which succeeded there could just as well cover the world. This little seed is one that everyone and everybody can propagate and transfer, and so they spread it. They did it wisely. They began in the natural center – Jerusalem and then they went to the nearest circumference – Judea, and then they went over to their cousins; then they went abroad to all nations and all tribes. It is a beautiful story. It is one of aggressive work; how they began with the Eunuch of Ethiopia, a black man; how then they went to Cornelius of Cæsarea; how then they went out with Paul and Barnabas to Asia Minor, and then Greece and then Ephesus, and then Rome and then the great western nations of Spain, and intervening tribes and provinces, until at last he could say: "I have fully preached the Gospel of Christ." This must be the spirit of our Christianity. It must begin at

49

home and go out to all within the reach of our influence; but it must not stay here. It must reach out to all the highways and hedges of sin, but it must not stop there. It must go out over all the land where there is a hungry community wanting the fulness of Christ but it must not stop there until the tribes of Africa and India and the unevangelized nations of Europe and Asia, and the still remaining islands of the sea have all heard, at least, of Christ; perhaps not all been saved, but all have heard the message. There was a little church in Antioch that evangelized the world, and it was not as big as this when it began. There was a little church in Germany with a humble pastor named Harnis, and that man began to tell the people that one humble German church could evangelize the world, and that little church today has 12,000 Christian followers in the heart of Africa. There was another little church in Bohemia 200 years ago which began to send its members abroad and that church today has 70,000 members in foreign fields with only about a third as many at home. I mean the Moravians. I am sure that the spirit of aggressiveness, of unselfish work will be the power at home. May the dear Lord give to us this apostolic spirit. We are often told what has been done for modern missions; we think there is a great deal done, but I am sure it does not average as much as you give for your street car fare. Indeed, I suppose that most of you will spend more in the street cars today than the average amount expended to spread the Gospel through the world in a whole year by each of the Christians of America in obedience to the command: "Go ye into all the world and preach the Gospel to every creature."

V.

Again, another feature of apostolic Christianity, was prayer. They were born upon their knees; they were

50

baptized upon their knees. They were rebaptized in their second Pentecost in a prayer meeting. They went out to their mission work from their knees. Peter was delivered from prison and from prison and from Herod through the praying church. It was all prayer. So it must be with us.

VI.

Again, another feature was faith and hope and love. These three sweet jewels were the crown of the apostolic church. Faith in their testimony, faith in their salvation, faith in their work, sublime faith that attempted great things for God and expected great things from God. Stephen was full of faith, the great and good Barnabas was a man full of faith and the Holy Ghost. There is no credit in this. It is a ridiculous thing to talk about George Mueller as a prodigious example of faith; it is a ridiculous thing that you should wonder when any one possesses much faith. It is only your duty, and to look upon anybody that believes in God as a matter of surprise shows that you have a very, a very poor opinion of God, and it is lowering the standard of Christian faith. God expects you to believe as much as He expects you to be holy, and He gives as well as claims this faith from us.

Again hope is the second of this trinity of graces. We find hope in the apostolic churches more than we do in any church today. Hope, I mean, of the Lord's Second Coming. That was the very first message that God gave them. "Ye men of Galilee, why stand ye gazing up into Heaven? This same Jesus which is taken up from you into Heaven, shall so come in like manner as ye have seen Him go into Heaven;" and they never forgot that message. They saw Him go up and they were looking for Him to come back again, the same way, and that encouraged them in their work as they waited for His Son from Heaven. Their hope was His glorious appearing. O, I thank God that this glorious apostolic hope is dawning like a sun of righteousness in these days. Out of these beautiful windows, it seems to me, I have seen these past days and weeks, as I have never seen before, the star in the East and dawning of the advent glory and the mighty procession of the coming King – how near I do not know, how near I do not need to know, but that it is near I know. It is this blessed hope that makes the work so easy and the recompense so glorious. O, let us feel as though He had gathered us together at a recruiting station for His return, and let us gather around and be found ready to welcome Him.

Then the third feature of the church was love. Faith hope and love. What wondrous love they had. They were all of one heart. There was no self there. Barnabas brought his wealth and laid it down at the feet of Christ. He got the crown of usefulness and went out as an evangelist and as a blessing to the church. Mary, of Jerusalem, gave her house for prayer meetings, and the church met there, and Stephen gave his blood as freely as Paul gave his tongue. They gave themselves wholly to God. There was perfect Christian fellowship, and they upheld with loving unison each other's hearts. They went to the work hand in hand and heart to heart. They shared their blessings and trials, and were united against the common enemy. We love our pastor, perhaps, and we love the Lord, and we love the church, but we do not care much about one another. There is very little fellowship, very little unity of hearts in modern churches.

If you are determined to be a loving Christian, if you have set your face like a flint, you will love in spite of discouragements, and you will find that everybody will love you. It will be magnetic. We must love if we are to be an apostolic church. We must cease to say mine and thine and belong only to Him who owns us all, and for His dear sake we must "provoke one another to love and good works."

VII.

Finally, the last feature was suffering. It came soon. As soon as they got the power it had to be burned in. There had to be trial; there must be much misunderstanding if we are to obey the Holy Ghost and preach apostolic testimony – an apostolic life.

These early servants of God were not only blamed for their goodness – they were blamed for much that was false and much that was evil. They were put to death – glorious women and glorious men – under charges of the most horrible crimes, which everybody believed; but they went on with their faces toward God and their hearts full of love, and God understood them, and the world understands them today, and in the great day they will shine like the sun in the Kingdom of their Father.

O, beloved, we must not mind the pressure that comes from an unfriendly world. The pressure from even our fellow-Christians cannot hurt the work of God. If you are going to wait until men bolster you up there will be very little done. Come yourself and meet their questioning with a pressure of love and power from within, and God will give the vindication

When the traveler on the prairies finds that the flames are coming to meet him, he gathers a little circle around his camp and then he sets the dry grass on fire and sends it out to meet the other fire; away in the distance comes rushing in a wall of flame like an army rushing to meet him; his little wall widens and widens, until, at last, it meets the angry circle in the distance and overcomes it, and there is nothing left to burn. It cannot come any further; the traveler is saved by the fire that went from his own camp and his own hand; and so when the devil presses from without and the difficulties come from within send forth the fire of the Holy Spirit's blessed presence and our consecrated love and service. Let it go forth to meet the pressure of the world, and we shall find

53

that God is mightier than every difficulty, and that the very things that seem to be difficulties shall prove only a furtherance of the Gospel of Christ.

Dear friends, extremes always meet, and the first and last stages of Christianity are about to meet. The Spirit of Pentecost is to come back in the last days, and then the Master Himself is to come back as He went away. God has permitted you and me to live in these times. O, let us be like the men of Issachar of old "who had understanding of the times to know what Israel ought to do." Let us go back to Pentecost, let us go back to Olivet, let us go back to Calvary, and there let us wait His coming.

THE LAME MAN AT THE BEAUTIFUL GATE

CILICIA, THE BIRTHPLACE OF PAUL

CHAPTER IV.

CHRISTIAN LIFE IN THE EPISTLE TO THE ROMANS

"From faith to faith." – Rom. 1:17.

A PERSON recently asked me what was the best treatise that I could recommend on Christian life. I thought a little, and then I was obliged to say that the best book that I knew was the Epistle to the Romans, and then, perhaps, next to it, the Epistle to the Ephesians and the Gospel of John. They are all distinct treatises; there is no resemblance except in the general principles taught. In the Bible we have a score of books on Christian life, but it you look for the ideas of others they are not half so clear or full, and they will only give you a phase view of the Christian life at the best. As I have said sometimes to my own people, I never had any rest in my Christian life until I gave up trying to be like Fenelon or Baxter, or some other very good man, and simply took God's Word and tried to be like Christ and to have Christ in me, and I tell you today that I don't know of any book in the world as clear, and logical, and systematic, and spiritual as the New Testament. We go away back to Chrysostom. Why don't we go back to Paul and read his letters as if they were little books, divide treatises – as they, indeed, are – and I would not give this one for all the volumes of systematic theology that were ever written. This Epistle to the Romans is the systematic theology of the Bible; it is the only one of the books that has the complete, logical system in it; it is complete; it is like a good architectural edifice with its foundations laid away down in the rock or the concrete, and then proportionately carried up to the highest point – to the crowning point – where all is dedicated to the glory of Christ.

It is not my purpose this morning to analyze the epistle in a very explicit manner. You will find in Romans five or six great themes that are exhaustive and complete. The first of these is the question of the DIVINE existence. The apostle proves that most conclusively. Then he takes up the question of SIN, which comes next, you know, in our theological treatises. Then comes SALVATION. When he has got people down on their faces he takes up the question of salvation, and in the third, fourth and fifth chapters he shows us how we are saved through the redemption of Jesus Christ. It says more in a few words than any composition I have ever read. Then comes the question of SANCTIFICATION, and that is very fully discussed in the next three chapters (sixth, seventh and eighth). If you want to be a true Christian read those three chapters. Then comes the next question, namely: God's great purpose in dwelling with men. We are not fit to talk about that until we get sanctified.

When we get as far as the eighth chapter of Romans then he takes you through the ninth, tenth and eleventh, which discuss God's great plans and purposes in dealing with nations and men, and you can not understand them until you can look at them from the standpoint of your own salvation. It is all wrong to talk about them to unsaved men; but when you get up to the heights of the great salvation you can look down and say: "O, the depth of the wisdom and the knowledge of God." It is a view from the mountain top which you can not stand until your heart is prepared by these earlier chapters. Then the last great theme is the theme of CONSECRATED SERVICE. In the twelfth chapter we have the keynote of that, and in the following chapters it is developed in great beauty and completeness. Such is the Epistle to the Romans. God's being; our fallen state; salvation through Jesus Christ;

58

sanctification through union with Jesus and the Holy
Ghost; God's great purposes for us and others; and
service, consecration to Jesus and His work – these are
its great themes.

Now, then, having glanced at the structure of this
wonderful letter of Paul, I want this morning to dwell a
little on this one point. What kind of a Christian life does
it unfold for you and me? What are the great principles
that it brings out for us to build our characters upon and
to grow up into all the possibilities of a follower and a
reproduction of Jesus Christ. This word that I have read
this morning is the keynote. "The Gospel is the power of
God unto salvation to every one that believeth." The
idea of this epistle is power through believing the power
that comes into our life by faith in God and in the Word
of God. This thought of power was our theme last
Sabbath morning in the Acts of the Apostles. "Ye shall
receive power." And I think many of us, I think all of us
felt very much humbled as we thought of the
ineffectiveness of much of our Christian life and I
believe that we have been deeply longing for Divine
power. Today it is power again, but not in the same
aspect; not so much in the Holy Ghost as through faith.
Faith is the secret of power, of salvation, of purity, of
service, of everything that is worth having; power *to
every one that believeth.* There is the secret of this
epistle in its application to Christian life. "From faith to
faith." The Epistle to the Romans is a ladder, and its
rungs are separate degrees of faith, from faith to faith.
You begin with faith and you go on with faith, and you
go up with faith, and it is faith all the way to the end. It
is just a gradation of faith, and he that enters into its
completeness, just goes from faith to faith. Most people
go from faith, but they don't go to any other faith. The
very first step with faith dear friends, that you take is to
another step, and from that to another. Every mountain
top that is gained just brings into your vision another

59

mountain top beyond, and when you reach that, supposing it to be the highest pinnacle, you find towering peaks beyond, and so on to the eternal ascension. That is what this epistle means, from faith to faith, and that is what Christian life means.

Many people think, once we are saved, we will not have any more struggles of faith, but then our trials of faith begin. I suppose sometimes you think if you get through this difficulty you will never have any more, but you find the moment you are successful that you have a harder trial and must have mightier faith, and so you struggle on from faith to faith. This epistle leads us along the ladder of faith, and we find that every new step of our Christian life comes by another act of faith.

I. – JUSTIFIED BY FAITH.

First, we are justified by faith. I need not dwell very much on this, because I hope most of you have got beyond it.

A few years ago Dr. James, of Albany, wrote a book called "Grace for grace," which was read by nearly all the earnest-minded Christian people in this land. He was a Presbyterian minister who had got a little nearer to the Lord than his brethren, and in his latter years became a teacher of Christian life; so that he was occupied during his last years with this form of ministry. He wrote this book just before he passed away, giving his experience in dealing with these various people, and he said that he had found in almost every instance that the reason people had difficulties about the deeper Christian life was because they had not a clear assurance of their justification; they were not justified fully by faith; they were justified partly by faith and partly by works and partly by feeling, but as soon as their feelings changed and their purposes of doing good became a little weak their assurance would cease. The result was they could not make any progress;

60

they could not know Christ as a satisfying Presence and sanctifying power.

So it is, dear friends; and if you are not getting on very well on the upper rungs of the ladder you have got a break somewhere in the lower rung, and you had better read over the first, second, third and fourth chapters of Romans again, and see how you stand in reference to that. They teach us, first of all, that our justification is not pardon, not blotting out your old record and leaving it blank, but it is putting God's righteousness to your credit. He never calls it pardon, but He always calls it righteousness with God. God does not pardon you and say: "Yes, I won't punish you; I will let that go." He does not merely let you out of prison and leave you at the door, but He puts on you His own righteousness and makes you stand as well as if you were the holiest being in the universe, stand as well as His own Son stands in His sight. That is God's righteousness. When God takes a poor sinner He puts him into the place of Jesus, His Son, and accepts him as Jesus is accepted. "Wherein He hath made us accepted in the beloved." This is the name whereby He shall be called Jehovah Tiskenu. He does not merely pass by our sin and rub it out and wait to see how long it will be until we fill up the score again, but He puts on us a robe of immaculate whiteness, and puts to our credit an account which makes us worthy in the worthiness of Christ. Now, that is how it is that we can ask things in confidence.

Two young girls came to my office and asked me if I would pray for them. I said: "Why cannot you ask for yourselves?" and they said: "Why, we are not worthy to ask for ourselves," and then they told me about a dear friend and cousin of theirs, and one of them said: "The Major could ask things from God, because he is good, but I could not ask so much." I said: "God would not give Major anything because he is so good. If He gives him anything it is because He has put to his credit His

61

own righteousness. If he should ask for anything according to his own merits he would be cast out a poor, undeserving sinner, and so would I." Then I said: "Suppose you had a kind friend visiting you in New York, who was pretty well off, and after she was here two or three weeks she should say: 'I am going to leave $200 with Mr. Macy for you to purchase goods, whatever you wish;'" I said: "Suppose you should go down there, you would not say: 'I would not dare to buy a hundred dollars' worth here; I will buy four or five dollars' worth.' Who would get the benefit of that except Mr. Macy? Why, he would say to you: 'This money is paid, the same as if you had paid it; it is to your credit, and you are very foolish if you don't get the benefit of it.' Now, you are entitled to two hundred dollars' worth, and I will venture to say that you would not let any of that hundred dollars be lost, but it would all be claimed to the last cent, and you would feel that you were entitled to it, although you hadn't paid a penny yourself. That is the way we go to God. We have nothing to present to Him as a claim, but on the books of God to our credit the infinite righteousness of Christ has been deposited, and God comes and says, in His name, ask my help as far as that credit will go. You have not any right, but He has a right, and He gives it to you." "Oh!" she says, "I see it. Why, I think I could ask anything of God now." Now, dear friends, that is the meaning of justification; it is not that you are pardoned, and slipped through on sufferance. That is not very creditable; but you are lifted right up into the peace of Jesus Himself, and you stand where He stands. The very moment after you have come to Him He puts you in His place and represents you to the Father. Now, that is justification. We are made righteous through the righteousness of Christ. There is no difference between Major and his little cousin; no difference between George Muller and you, poor sinners.

Both are perfectly justified as much as Christ is the moment you accept Jesus as your righteousness.

The next thought is about faith in connection with this justification. I must give a moment to this. What is this faith that brings us our justification? Well, the apostle tells us in the fourth chapter of Romans. He explains faith far better than any modern exposition of faith. He tells us about Abraham. He says Abraham was the father of believers and their pattern. If you want to know how to believe for anything just go back to Abraham. How did Abraham believe? This is the way Abraham believed: "He believed God who quickeneth the dead, and calleth those things that be not as though they were, who against hope believed in hope. Being not weak in faith he considered his own body now dead. When he was about a hundred years old he staggered not at the promise of God, but was strong in faith, giving glory to God, being fully persuaded that what He had promised He was able also to perform." That was faith. That was Abraham's faith nearly four thousand years ago, and that must be your faith still. Faith is believing God strongly enough to call the thing so, even when it is not so. He calleth the things that are not as though they were. If God says so, it is so. It is staggering not at the promise, as you and I so often have staggered through unbelief and thought it was an impossible thing to do. We call it our misfortune. God calls it unbelief. Abraham believed against hope, in the face of every probability. When everything looked the other way he considered not appearances; he considered not his own body. It was dead. That didn't make any difference, if God said it. He considered not his own body, now dead, nor any of the circumstances; and he did not even stagger, but was strong in faith, and fully persuaded that God would fulfil His promise, and he called it by its new name, and let the world know that he accepted that which looked like foolishness. That is faith. God said: "You are going to

63

have a child named Isaac, and through him all the promises are to come. You are to be the father of multitudes of nations." He did not hesitate a minute. He believed God. "Do you really believe me?" God seemed to ask: "Are you willing to let the world know you believe? Well, then, take a new name that will signify this. Then take the name Abraham, 'the father of a multitude.'" Abraham didn't stop to say: "They will laugh at me; they will ridicule me;" but he just obeyed and waited until God vindicated his trust and the fulfillment came, and it is coming still, and it will be coming until the end of time and the ages of eternity; because Abraham believed God without sight. That is faith; but to believe a thing, anything, when it seems easy and probable is not faith; to reason it out and say: "It must be so, because I have proved it so," is not faith; to get a great lot of probabilities heaped up and build your house on it and say this man is back of it and that man is back of it; there is so much influence and money, and it has got to come. That is not faith. But when it looks like a forlorn hope, when there is no probability, to stand and say: "In the name of the Lord I go forward, and He cannot fail." "Blessed is he that hath not seen and yet hath believed."

Now, that is the way man is justified. He just believes God like Abraham. He comes to the feet of God a poor sinner, nothing in him, and God says: "Forgiven," and he believes. God says: "My child;" he says: "My Father." He does not feel it, does not see it, but just believes it. When you do that you are saved the moment you believe. The great trouble with people is they want to have some inward sign, some pleasant sensation, some outside proof, something in their life which shows it; but God says you must believe without sight, and when you do it is counted to you for righteousness. That is the way you get peace with God, and then having got salvation in that way you are ready to go on and get all other things in the same way. It is not your weeping, your working or your straining, it is your trusting that brings you peace. If there is any man or woman here this morning that is unsaved, in His great name I bid you believe today and rest in His great word; and, until you do, you will never be at rest. Then having settled this question and rested your trouble on His word, you can go forth and serve Him and work for Him "Therefore, being justified by faith, we have peace with God through our Lord Jesus Christ, by whom we also have access also by faith into this grace wherein we stand and rejoice in the hope of the glory of God, and we joy in God through our Lord Jesus Christ, by whom we have now received the Atonement."

II. – SANCTIFIED BY FAITH.

Now, glance next at the subject of SANCTIFICATION by faith. In the sixth chapter he tells us that you cannot sanctify your old nature. You cannot sanctify the man who was born of his mother any more than you can sanctify the devil. You cannot make a bad man good; you cannot make your bad heart pure. Beloved, this is the fatal error that people are making through the church. They are trying to sanctify the flesh. He said He would take away the old heart. "I will take away the hard and stony heart, and I will give you a heart of flesh." God does not cleanse the old heart. It must die out and be put aside. So this sixth chapter of Romans begins with this first word: We are buried with Christ in baptism unto death. Reckon therefore yourself to be dead indeed unto sin; put aside your own evil nature as a hopeless business; reject it, and come to Him for the nature born from above. A great many people try to believe with their own heart; they cannot believe; there is no believing in it. There is nothing in it but doubt and fear. It is a serpent, and it will hiss like a serpent until it is trodden under the heel of Jesus. A great many people try to love and forgive with their own heart, but they cannot. You must reject it and get a new spirit from God. So the first step in sanctification is to die to your own self and count it useless, hopeless and helpless, judge yourself capable of all sin, and say: "Lord, in my flesh there dwelleth no good thing." If you do not believe it I will tell you what will happen. You will find it out by a very discouraging process and by a desperate failure. I never saw anybody yet who doubted this doctrine who could meet the issue. Happy they that take Him at His word and get His righteousness in lieu of their own.

It is not enough to die to yourself. You must rise now. You are not only dead, but you have arisen with Jesus Christ's resurrection life. Where am I to get the faith, and the love and the goodness? Out of my heart? No. Where? Out of the risen Christ. Where shall I look then? Why, look to Him. Looking off unto Jesus, the Author and Finisher of our faith. It is union with Jesus that is the source of all goodness in you. This is the secret of the Christian life.

Then the seventh chapter of Romans tells us how Paul was brought to experience this himself. He had an experience. He started out in the old way and tried to be good in his own strength; tried to sanctify his own heart, and he thought that he would do it by the law – by codes and rules. Some people believe in rules. I began with rules, but I was afraid to read them over after awhile, and soon I thought they were so terribly broken up that I would not try again. Rules won't save or sanctify you. Paul said he would get sanctified by taking these commandments and obeying them, but the commandments slew him. The Lord says: "You shall not;" and Paul says; "Who says I shall not." The Lord says: "You shall not;" and Paul says: "I shall." The Lord says: "You won't have this gratification," and he says: "I must have it." That is the way nature works. The very moment you say it must not, it says it must. The law

66

only raised up the old evil heart and made it worse than ever, and at last he died. He gave up in despair. "O, wretched man that I am! Who shall deliver me from this body of death? I have not a thing in me but is like a corpse. I tried to shake it off, but it won't go. It wraps around me like a shroud. How shall I get rid of it?" That was Paul's experience.

I read somewhere of a sailor who went to dive under the sea, and he felt something very soft in the bottom, and it seemed to touch every part of his body, and at last he found himself just suffocating in the arms of a monster. He pulled the bell, and was drawn to the surface; when he got there a hideous jellyfish had thrown about him a hundred hands and was embracing him to a horrible death. When the sailors saw it they shrieked out in fear. It was just as if death had embraced him in its bosom. O, that is the way this old heart appears before us when we see it in God's light – a horrid death, and we say: "O, wretched man that I am, who Shall deliver me from this body of death!" One of the sailors, who had a little more presence of mind than the others, poured a phial of strong acid over the horrid thing, and in a moment it disengaged itself and dropped into the sea. Had he fought with it, he would have become entangled more in its toils; and so the apostle says: "Who shall deliver me from this body of death?" In a moment comes the answer: "I THANK GOD THROUGH JESUS CHRIST." He stops trying; he just looks up and trusts his Lord. Jesus touches him with His love, with His spirit, and henceforth it is no longer Paul's battle with himself, but it is Christ's battle with the old Paul and with the old Satan, and Jesus is his captain and conqueror, to deliver from his inward life as well as for his outward and his eternal.

O, beloved, have not you tried this battle in your own hearts, and have not you found the more you tried the worse it grew. O, this day let it pass into the hands of

67

Christ. Jesus has come to save you from your inward soul, from your old self. He is the sanctification of the heart as well as the atonement for the soul, and if you will just commit it to Him He will be to you this new life and purity forever; and you shall live by faith, sanctified as well as justified through Jesus only.

And then, in the eighth chapter, he tells us a little more about it. He goes one step further, and reveals to us the glorious fact that the Holy Ghost now comes as the Spirit of Jesus to dwell in the heart, and take charge of the battle for Christ and for us. O, how precious and beautiful the teachings here about this Spirit's work. He says: "The law of the Spirit of Life in Christ Jesus hath made us free from the law of sin and death." It is not your own efforts, but it is the Spirit of Life in Christ that does it; the Holy Spirit, as the Spirit who dwelt in Christ and brings Christ's life.

Then, again, he makes us to be spiritually minded, for "the minding of the spirit is life and peace." It is a life of peace and blessing when the mind of the Spirit just dwells within you.

Again, he says, if this Spirit dwell in you, "He also quickens your mortal bodies by His Spirit that dwelleth in you." That is, that He shall give you Divine life and healing. It is He who quickens our nerves and renews our strength. It is the Holy Ghost that comes into the man, comes into his heart and makes of it sweet and pure, comes into his head and makes it clear, comes into his nerves and makes them cool and vigorous, and thus purifies your soul and quickens your mortal bodies by the Spirit that dwelleth in you.

Then, again, he says He leads us. "As many as are led to the Spirit are the sons of God." He witnesses that you are a child. He prays for you. We know not how to pray as we ought, but the Spirit prays in us "with groanings which cannot be uttered. Then the epistle rises to still greater heights. The ladder mounts away up this glorious

68

elevation until it is lost on the mountain tops of eternity, as he cries, all things work together for good to them that love God. Who is he that condemeth? who shall separate us from the love of Christ? It is all clear now, because faith has taken the place of self, and Jesus Christ is all and in all for His people, present and future.

III. – CONSECRATED BY FAITH.

In the third place, faith consecrates us. Now, there is a great deal of consecration by works, by efforts, and in the spirit of slavery and fear, a great deal of giving one's self to God because we ought to do it, but would rather not do it, a great deal of dedicating to God of that which is unwilling, which has to be chained on the altar, and even then does not lie very still. But true consecration is this: "I beseech you by the mercies of God that you present your bodies a living sacrifice, holy and acceptable unto God." That is the spirit of consecration, drawn by the mercies of God, willingly, heartily the sacrifice offered by your own hands and your own free choice, because of God's love for you, because He has saved you, because He has sanctified you, because He will never leave you and never forsake you. These cords are silken, but there is no resisting and no trying to pull away, but you lie on that altar, glad to be there, feeling it only a privilege to be all the Lord's. That is consecration of faith.

First, you do it for love's sake and not for duty. Secondly, you do it not to be saved, but because you are saved. Further, you do it believing that you are accepted and that God does take you, and is really, truly, fully yours, and you surely and eternally His.

In the heart of Africa, it is related by an Englishman, that a slave procession passed by, and the King called out a poor slave who displeased him in some little way, ordered his men to put their arrows to their bowstrings and avenge the offence with his blood. He went up to the native chief and begged for the poor slave's life, offered him a great deal of money and costly bribes, but the chief turned to him and said: "I don't want ivory, or slaves, or gold; I can go against yonder tribe and capture their stores and their villages; I want no favors from the white man; all I want is blood." Then he ordered one of his men to pull his bowstring and discharge an arrow at the heart of the poor slave. The young man, with the instinct of a moment, threw himself in front and held up his arm and the next moment the arrow was quivering in the flesh of his own arm. The black man was astonished. Then he pulled the arrow from his arm, and the blood flowed, and he said to the chief: "Here is blood; here is my blood; I give it for this poor slave, and I claim his life." The native chief had never seen such a spectacle before, and he was completely overcome by it. He gave the slave to the white man. He said: "Yes, white man has bought him with his blood, and he shall be yours." In a moment the poor slave threw himself at the feet of his deliverer, tears flowing down his face, and said: "O, white man, you have bought Lebe with your blood; Lebe" (for that was his name) "shall be your slave forever and ever," and ever after he could not make him take his liberty; wherever he went, poor Lebe was beside him; no drudgery was too hard, no task too hopeless. He was bound by the mercy of his deliverer as his consecrated servant. O, friends, if a poor savage heart can thus be bound by the wound of a stranger's arm, what should you and I say for those deeper wounds in those two living hands and feet and the heart that was opened by the spear? If we believe that we are redeemed how can we but be consecrated to Him.

Now, when this is done, these last chapters of Romans will become our experience; this beautiful picture of consecration will come into your daily life. And what is it? Just for a moment gaze into this looking glass and see the face that you ought to have, if you have not got it

70

now. First, he says: "Not conformed to this world, but transformed." If you are consecrated to God by faith, you will not count it hard to give up the world. You will say: "How can I love the world and obey my Lord?" You cannot be persuaded to love the world apart from Jesus. You will be not conformed, but transformed. That is the very first step in consecration – separation from the world. Then, the next step is great humility – "not to think of yourself more highly than you ought to think" – dependent every moment on Him. The next step is mutual service with respect to one another; many members in one body, but all one and considering each other, and each one filling his place. The next is public and active service for Christ – the various forms of ministry. "He that giveth, he that exhorteth" – the services and activities of a thorough Christian life. And, next, are the social duties of life. Consecrated people will always be loving, obliging, sympathetic and kind. Then, the next is: Love to your enemies, forgiving them, and heaping coals of fire on their heads. The consecrated man is one of those of whom God says nothing shall offend. "They that love thy law nothing shall offend." A consecrated Christian ought never to be offended. Then, the next chapter tells us that if we are consecrated, we shall be right in our civil duties, in our relations to the state; there will not be strifes and troubles with others. I don't think we will have lawsuits; I don't think we will have labor difficulties; I do not think we will get into a tangle with others, but go through life good citizens, bringing our religion into our business and all the relationships of life.

Then, the thirteenth and fourteenth chapters tell us about this consecration making us patient with weak Christians and when we see others a little strange; when we hear things that are a little trying they will not disturb us; we will show that we are strong by bearing the infirmities of the weak. I tell you, friends, that is

71

consecration: separation from the world, serving the Lord, living in love, forgiving your enemies, a good citizen, a righteous merchant and a patient Christian with the weakest, most trying and most peculiar people we come in contact with.

And the last chapter is a picture of the many forms of this consecrated service in the work of Christ. Paul's service comes in: "I have fully preached the Gospel of Christ." Phoebe's service comes in – our sister Phoebe – "a servant of the church at Cenechrea;" Priscilla and Aquilla come in "who have for me laid down their necks, and to whom the church of God gives thanks. And Persis, too, "who labored much in the Lord."

All these are types of service and pages from the eternal record. The only power that can bring us to this consecration, is the "faith that works by love." All the power in the world could not raise that iceberg one foot, but one day of sunshine can lift it up high in the air, and turn it into a floating mass of transfigured glory in the clouds of heaven. So all your trying and your doing cannot consecrate you, but one really believing conception of His love can make all your life one living, loving sacrifice.

CHAPTER V.

CHRISTIAN LIFE IN FIRST CORINTHIANS

PART I. – LIFE IN JESUS

"Of Him are ye in Christ who of God is made unto you wisdom, even righteousness, sanctification and redemption." – 1Cor. 1:30.

*T*HE boast of the cultured Greeks, (and the Corinthians were Greeks), was their WISDOM. *Sophia* they called it, and we call it philosophy. So highly did they value the esthetic and intellectual, that many of them became disgusted with Paul on account of the simplicity and crudeness of his preaching, and formed a new party around Apollos, the learned philosopher of Alexandria. Paul could have given them philosophy, too, but he determined to know nothing among them but Christ and Him crucified. He knew all their sophies and circles, but he knew also their little worth and he brought a *Sophia* as far transcending them all as the clear sunlight excels the brilliant fireworks of the night. This is his philosophy: "We preach Christ, the wisdom of God;" "God hath made foolish the wisdom of the world, but of Him are ye in Christ who of God is made unto us WISDOM." And then, to show the elements and constituents of this wisdom he adds: "that is even righteousness, sanctification and redemption." Our wisdom, our science, our philosophy is Christ the

73

incarnate, crucified, risen Son of God; and Christ is to us wisdom in meeting the three greatest needs of our being namely: "righteousness, sanctification and redemption."

Now, you will notice the first difference between God's wisdom and man's, is that the one is a theory, the other is a Person. How often in human councils, after a dozen have talked about it, one strong spirit suddenly rises up and does it. William the Silent and Oliver Cromwell were worth a hundred thousand talkers. So the Greeks were mere talkers. The best of them had nothing better than beautiful theories, but could not save the world. God did something. He sent His Son, and He came to talk about deliverance after He had brought it. And so still, the whole Gospel is summed up in the Person of Jesus. It is not His perfect law. His wise and holy directions for living. His gracious promises. His wondrous plan of mercy. His incomparable method of saving us and sanctifying us, or even His most precious gifts and helps that we most prize, but at every point He is constantly giving us Himself, and meeting every need and difficulty in His own person, and being made unto us of God our wisdom, our righteousness, sanctification and redemption.

> "He did not send
>   But came Himself to save;
> His help He did not lend
>   But His own self He gave."

Again, the wisdom of God is practical and meets the real and most vital needs of our life. These three words sum up the whole of our spiritual need. Righteousness meets the awful question of guilt and judgment. Sanctification provides against the deep and desperate power and dominion of sin; and redemption covers all the field of Satan's power over our body, our spiritual conflicts, and our future inheritance.

74

I. – CHRIST IS OUR RIGHTEOUSNESS.

RIGHTNESS will convey the best idea of the meaning of this word in this connection. It means the adjusting and making right of our relations with God. This is more than mere pardon. It implies a complete settlement of all God's claims and full satisfaction for all our disobedience. It puts us back in the position of righteous persons as fully as if we had ourselves paid every debt and kept every precept of the law.

Now, this comes to us not only through the work, but especially through the person of Christ. He is made unto us righteousness. That is, He unites us to Himself, and puts us in the very position which He Himself occupies. He is perfect righteousness and we become so one with Him, and take Him so into us that we are "made the righteousness of God in Him." It is not quite the same as if a slave were bought and set free, but rather as if the master should wed his slave and take her up into his own very being, station and rank. Christ not only redeems us. He becomes unto us righteousness. He so takes us into Himself that we stand related to the Father Just exactly as He does – "Accepted in the Beloved;" that is accepted as the Beloved.

Once, on a wintry night, Napoleon was walking over his camp, when he found a sentinel asleep. The penalty was death. But Napoleon snatched up the soldier's musket and took his place on the beat, and paced the round for two hours, until the sentinel awoke with a start, looked up and saw the emperor, and then fell at his feet and begged for his life. The emperor simply handed him back his musket, and passed on. He saved him by standing in his place. It is thus we are justified. Christ makes common cause with us, and stands where we failed, and we are counted as if we had done what He has done for us. "There is therefore now no condemnation to them that are in Christ Jesus."

II. – CHRIST OUR SANCTIFICATION.

Sanctification is the deeper work which follows justification and deals directly with the inherent state of the heart with a view to its complete deliverance from the dominion and power of sin. God has made provision for this also, and God requires it of us all. It is not left until the hour of death or the entrance of the soul to Heaven, but is the work of life, and must be accomplished here. It is not our own work, for we are as helpless to sanctify ourselves as to make an atonement for our sins. It is part of Christ's redemption, and one of the free gifts of His grace, and, like our justification, it must come to us through Christ Himself. It is not a character slowly built up in us. It is not a subjective state created in us and then stereotyped and crystallized for life. "Christ is made unto us sanctification." He does not give us a certain measure and quantity of sanctity, but He gives us His own holy presence to keep our heart like His own. It is somewhat like the case of a bankrupt who applies to you for ten thousand dollars to save his business. You do not give him the ten thousand dollars and leave him to work it out himself, but you give him yourself and all your capital, and experience, and standing, and brains to carry him and his business henceforth, coming in as a partner, and carrying all the responsibilities for and with him.

So Jesus comes into the surrendered heart, identifying and uniting Himself with it, imparting to it His own life and being, and becoming anew, from day to day, the supply of its spiritual needs and the substitute for its helplessness. Our part is therefore simply to yield ourselves and fully recognize our own nothingness; and, then, take Jesus Himself to live in us and be, moment by moment, our strength, purity and victory. We need rest,

76

and we take Him to fill us with His peace. We need love, and we take His heart of love to rule in our breast and, moment by moment, overcome all bitterness, selfishness and sin. We need faith, we take Him to fill us ever with His own trust, so that the life we now live in the flesh we shall "live by the faith of the Son of God." We are tempted, He in us will meet the temptation and be our shield. Instead of our own wayward and wandering thoughts, "we have the mind of Christ." Instead of our own wavering faith we have "the faith of God." Instead of our own evanescent emotions, we have "His Joy to remain in us and our joy is full." Instead of our self-perfection, we have a perfect Christ and are "complete in Him." Instead of our own life it is "not I, but Christ that liveth in me." Instead of our becoming something we are nothing, and He is All in all. Instead of getting IT we are getting HIM; instead of a thing, a glorious person; instead of a personal state, a divine presence and a living, loving, all-sufficient Lord. We shall never feel strong again. But we shall ever have His strength to fall back on. We shall never be satisfied with ourselves, but "in Him all our wants are supplied; His love makes our Heaven below." We shall never be sufficient any more for anything, but He will ever keep saying: "My grace is sufficient for thee;" and we shall answer ever back: "Our sufficiency is of God."

Thus we shall ever be kept dependent upon and abiding in Him. "As the branch cannot bear fruit of itself except it abide in the vine, no more can ye except ye abide in Me." Thus our continual purity will come through constant abiding, for "He that abideth in Him sinneth not." And thus our power and victory will ever be linked with the most helpless dependence upon His might and get as great as His omnipotence, and daring ever to claim: "I can do all things through Christ that strengtheneth me."

This is the Gospel of full salvation. This is not human, but divine holiness. This is the true secret of sanctification. It is simply JESUS. It lays us in the dust and silences all our boasting, and then it lifts us up to the Heavens, and gives us a holiness as much higher than Adam's unfallen state, or the highest human perfection, as God is higher than man; and the perfection of Christ transcends the most perfect mortal. Glory be to Jesus forever, made unto us of God sanctification.

How shall we enter in. Give up ourselves, truly willing to be sanctified wholly, and fully recognizing our helplessness, and then take Jesus for our whole spiritual life and need, and keep taking and drawing upon Him afresh every moment in a union so intimate, and a dependence so absolute, that you can say: "I live, yet not I, but Christ liveth in me."

III. – CHRIST OUR REDEMPTION.

The word redemption implies deliverance from an oppressor by a ransom. It is to receive its highest and grandest fulfillment in the final and complete deliverance of our bodies from the power of death in the resurrection, and the glorious inheritance of the future kingdom. It is for this that "the whole creation groaneth and travaileth in pain together until now, waiting for the adoption, to wit, *the redemption,* of the body." Then, indeed, in the fullest sense will Christ be made unto us redemption, as He clothes us with His own resurrection glory, and seats us with Him on His throne. But is there no sense in which this physical redemption begins here and anticipates the triumphs and glories of eternity? Have we not even now the earnest of our inheritance until the redemption of the purchased possession? Does not the apostle teach us in the very chapter which describes most sublimely the future resurrection, that we have even now "the first fruits of the Spirit," the beginning and

78

anticipation of it? And again, in 2Cor. 5 after speaking of the house not made with hands which awaits our body in that day, he declares that God hath given us the earnest of it now by the Spirit in our hearts.

Yes, the redemption of the body and its resurrection life begin to reach us even here. "If the Spirit of Him that raised up Jesus from the dead dwell in us. He that raised up Christ from the dead shall," even now, "quicken our mortal bodies by His Spirit that dwelleth in us." Christ has delivered the body from Satan's mortgage, and He does not wait till death to set it free. Even as early as the days of Job there were some who could take the place of the true interpreter with the sick and suffering, and say: "Deliver from going down to the pit, for I have found a ransom." That was physical redemption, and when the sufferer received it the promise followed. "His flesh shall be fresher than a child's; he shall return to the days of his youth." David sang of this physical redemption: "Bless the Lord, O, my soul, * * * who forgiveth all thine iniquities, who healeth all thy diseases, who REDEEMETH THY LIFE FROM DESTRUCTION." Isaiah said of it: "Surely He hath borne our sicknesses and carried our pains, and by His stripes we are healed." Matthew translates the same sweet promise in words more literal and personal still: "Himself took our infirmities and bare our sicknesses." Zechariah takes up the first note of redemption before His birth and says: "He hath visited and redeemed His people * * * that we being delivered from all our enemies and the hand of them that hate us might serve Him without fear in righteousness and holiness before Him all the days of our life."

Peter preached this gospel of redemption to the poor cripple at the Beautiful Gate, and Paul gave it to the impotent man at Lystra without fear of their pressing too far on in its fulness. And James tells all the sick to claim it as one of the impartial provisions of the Gospel of Christ.

This does not mean physical redemption in the complete sense in which we shall have it after the resurrection. It does not mean exemption from death or immortal life, but physical health for the *mortal* until life's' work is done. In this sense Christ has provided for the physical redemption of His children, and offers it to all who will receive Him first.

Now, just as it was Christ Himself who justified us and Christ Himself who was made unto us sanctification, so it is only by personal union with Him that we can receive this physical life and redemption. It is, indeed, not a touch of power upon our body which restores and then leaves it to the mere resources of natural strength and life for the future, but it is the vital and actual union of our mortal body with the risen body of our Lord Jesus Christ, so that His own very life comes into our frame and he is Himself made unto us strength, health and full physical redemption. O, it is glorious, indeed, that He who is alive forevermore will condescend to live in these houses of clay and thrill these members with His own glorious body. They who thus receive Him may know Him as none ever can who exclude Him from the bodies which He has made for Himself. This is one of the deep and precious mysteries of the Gospel. "The body is for the Lord and the Lord for the body." "Know you not that your body is the temple of the Holy Ghost, which is in you, which ye have of God, and ye are not your own, for ye are bought with a price; therefore, glorify God in your body, which is God's?" (Revised version).

This is the secret of Divine Healing. It is "Christ made unto us redemption." It is the life of Jesus in our mortal flesh. And it is so sacred that those who once receive it can never spend it on their own gratification, but must "henceforth live not unto themselves but unto Him that died for them and rose again."

80

Now, in this great threefold sense, Christ is our Wisdom. Is there on earth, in the teachings of the hoary past, or the theories of all the wise of every generation, a philosophy so simple, so practical, so mighty and so kind? Such a Wisdom might well fill Paul with holy enthusiasm and cast a shadow of contempt on all the sophistries of the world. It is, indeed, the balm of life, the bane of death, the bar of hell, the bliss of heaven and the benediction of humanity. Glory be to God for such a Christianity, for such a Christ. Let us all take Him. Let us take Him in all His fulness.

CHAPTER VI.

CHRISTIAN LIFE IN FIRST CORINTHIANS

PART II. – THE DEEPER WORK OF THE SPIRIT

*A*FTER having shown in the first chapter how completely our whole life is summed up in the person of Christ, the apostle proceeds to unfold the deeper things of God and to show that the wisdom of God is not only infinitely more practical and helpful than man's, but is also much deeper and higher. This leads him to a series of remarkable passages which unfold with singular power the relation of the Holy Spirit to our deeper Christian life.

I. – THE SPIRIT AS OUR TEACHER AND REVEALER.

In the second chapter and the sixth verse the apostle declares that for those whose minds are prepared and matured there is a deeper wisdom than the mere rudiments of the Gospel and in the following verses he expounds more fully the principles of this deeper revelation.

1. Spiritual truth is not discovered by natural methods of investigation. "Eye hath not seen, nor ear heard, nor have entered into the heart the things which God hath prepared for them that love Him." Not by the outward senses, nor even by the conceptions, intuitions or reasonings of the heart, are these things to be known.

"The natural" or psychical "man perceiveth not the things of the Spirit of God, neither can he know them, for they are spiritually discerned."

The mere intellect is not sufficient to fully grasp or appreciate the truths of the heavenly world – just as the sense of smell is of no use to judge colors by, or the mathematical faculty to read music. Therefore, all the reasonings of the skeptic are futile to bring him into the light of God. And therefore also the dogmatism of theology and its intellectual pride so often lead it to miss the spiritual fullness of the Scriptures; while humble and unschooled hearts, digging on their knees, find mines of hidden treasure everywhere.

2. The Holy Spirit is the great revealer of spiritual truth. First, in His Word, and then in the personal teachings of the Paraclete in our hearts, "God hath revealed them unto us by His Spirit." The Holy Spirit is the source of all we know of God; and He must also teach what He has revealed. It is not enough that He has given it to us in His Word. He must also interpret that word to our hearts. "He shall guide you into all truth and bring all things to your remembrance, whatsoever I have said unto you." "He shall take of mine and shall show it unto you." The reason there is so much error and controversy in the world is because so many are taught by mere human teachers or mere human principles of reasoning and not by the Holy Ghost. He does not teach us all at once, but as fast as we are able to learn and retain His lessons. Often he uses the fire of suffering to burn them into our souls. He lets some trial and need come into our life and then He shows us Christ as its supply, and uses it to unfold some deeper truth of His Word in a manner we never can forget. He gently *"guides* us into all truth."

3. But the Holy Spirit is not only our Teacher, He is also revealed to us in these verses as bringing a new capacity for learning, and a new mind to receive and
84

understand His teaching, even "the mind of Christ." Not only do we need new light but new eyes; not only a Divine Teacher but a Divine mind. Your little canary could not understand you it you were to sit down and teach it philosophy, because it has a canary's mind. No alphabet or culture could bring it up to it. Not so with a savage Zulu. He would not understand you at first, but you could bring him up to it because he has a human mind.

So the things of God no mortal mind can understand or be taught to understand. We must get the Divine mind *in us* to know with. We must get a new capacity that is able to measure up to the new truth. "The natural man," that is, literally, the psychical, "cannot understand the things of God." The most cultivated philosopher of Athens, Edinburgh or Boston, can no more take in the realities of God and the eternal world than a canary can understand the words of the same philosopher. His head is as much too small for it as a tape measure to span the ocean. Hence the failures of all human reasoning to discover Divine truth. Hence the skepticism or rationalism of many of earth's brightest minds. Hence the slowness of many noble Christian scholars to see the deeper spiritual truths of Divine Holiness and supernatural power which the humble believer knows and lives on. Hence it has been well said that before a man can know or have much of Christ he must be beheaded, and then headed up anew in Christ, "in whom are hid all the treasures of wisdom and knowledge." Hence, "if any man will be wise let him become a fool that he may be wise, for the wisdom of this world is foolishness with God."

Now, instead of our poor narrow, erring minds, the Holy Spirit is willing to bring to the humble and earnest heart THE MIND OF CHRIST," and so unite His glorious Person to our inner life that we shall see with His eyes, understand with His thoughts and know as He knows. There are three departments of our being, the spirit, soul

85

or mind and body, and for each of these the Lord Jesus gives us Himself. When we thus receive His mind we see His word intuitively, spiritual truth falls into our apprehension as light falls upon a healthy eye or water into thirsty lips. We know the truth, and we know it is the truth. We know Him and we know it is He. Our whole body is full of light and our whole being is filled with Him. Our convictions are not mere conclusions, but they are the assurances of our deepest spiritual consciousness. And we can say in this blessed fellowship with God and truth: "Eye hath not seen nor ear heard, neither have entered into the heart of man the things which God hath prepared for them that love Him, but God hath revealed them unto us by His Spirit." Now, we have received the Spirit that is of God that we may know the things that are freely given us of God." Now, what are these deeper things which God thus reveals to His spiritual children? Not, as many would falsely claim, the strange and strained revelations of curious and speculative things which merely gratify an idle curiosity and fleshly mind; not the secrets which belong to God and could do us no good if we knew them; not the hearts of our Christian brethren that we may sit in censorious judgment upon them in a spirit of judicial pride; not the wild and unhallowed mysteries of spiritualism and the unseen world; not the visions and prophesyings which some seem to value as the seals of a special sanctity and Spirituality; not these mere externals or counterfeits of spiritual things, but a deeper knowledge of the Person, work, life and heart of Jesus, of His fullness and grace, of His mystical union with us, and His glorious purposes, promises and provisions for His people. This is why the eyes of your understanding are to be enlightened, "that you may know what is the hope of His calling and the riches of the glory of His inheritance in the saints, and what is the exceeding greatness of His power to us ward who believe according to the working of His mighty

86

power which He wrought in Christ when He raised Him from the dead and set Him at His own right hand in heavenly places, far above all principality, and power, and might, and dominion, and every name that is named, not only in this world but also in that which is to come, and gave Him to be Head over all things to His church, which is His body, the fulness of Him, that filleth all in all."

And, again, in the same epistle, he prays that they may be "strengthened with might by the spirit in the inner man that Christ may dwell in your heart by faith, that ye being rooted and grounded in love may be able to comprehend with all saints what is the breadth and length and depth and height and to know the love of Christ that passeth knowledge, that ye may be filled with all the fulness of God."

And yet, again, in the Epistle to the Colossians (2:1-3) he breathes a similar prayer for their coming into the deeper things of Christ. "I would that ye know what conflict I have for you and for them at Laodicea, and for so many as have not seen my face in the flesh, that their hearts might be comforted, being knit together in love and unto all the riches of the full assurance of understanding to the acknowledgement of the mystery of God and of the Father and of Christ, in whom are hid all the treasures of wisdom and knowledge." "Let no man beguile you of your reward, intruding into those things which he hath not seen, vainly puffed up by his fleshly mind, and not holding the Head, (2:18-19). These are the deep things of God into which we may plunge without fear until we are lost even in an ocean of love.

II. – THE SPIRIT AS AN INDWELLING PRESENCE.

In the third chapter and seventeenth verse he says: "Know ye not that ye are the temple of God and that the Spirit of God dwelleth in you?" And, again, in the sixth chapter and the nineteenth verse we read: "Know ye not that your body is the temple of the Holy Spirit, which is in you, which ye have of God, and ye are not your own, for ye are bought with a price; therefore, glorify God in your body, which is God's." (Revised version). Here we have a twofold indwelling of God, viz., in the spirit and in the body. The indwelling of the Holy Ghost in the human spirit is quite distinct from the work of regeneration. In Ezekiel 36:26, they are most clearly distinguished. The one is described as the taking away of "the hard and stony heart and giving the heart of flesh," of the other it is said: "I will put my Spirit within you and cause you to walk in my statutes, and ye shall keep my judgments and do them." The one is like the building of the house, the other the owner moving in and making it his own personal residence. There is a great difference. A man may build a hundred houses, but only live in one or two. The residence depends on many considerations. God only makes that heart his continual home which is wholly yielded to His direction and control. Many would not be able to bear the residence of the Holy God in their hearts, for it is added: "If any man defile the temple of God him will God destroy, for the temple of God is holy, which temple ye are."

This indwelling of the Holy Spirit is God's seal upon the consecration of the soul. It is very blessed and glorious. It makes the heart a throne and the life a heaven. God is no longer far off, or prayer a reaching up to distant heights, but His presence fills the heart and whispers the response to the waiting soul. He brings the Father and the Son to abide within and fills the heart with the peace and holiness, the power and glory of God. This wondrous indwelling of God within us is the greatest dignity and mystery of the new Dispensation. Not in the Old Testament did God come so near. He came upon His ancient saints and servants but not in them. But over and over again swelled the notes of prophecy and promise. "Lo, I come and dwell in the midst of thee." "In that day it shall be said thy God in the midst of thee is mighty. He will joy over thee with singing." "I will dwell in them and walk in them and will be their God and they shall be my people."

And in the New Testament Christ announces the mystery of God as at length to be realized. "The Comforter," He says, "dwelleth with you (in me) AND SHALL BE IN YOU." And when the day of Pentecost was fully come it was at last fulfilled. The Spirit of God came in this Living Person to make His dwelling within the human heart, just as He had dwelt in Christ, and henceforth God was united to man even as He was to the Son of Man. "At that day ye shall know that I am in my Father and ye in Me and I in you."

O, what a dignity and sacredness this gives to the consecrated life. "Know you not that ye are the temple of God, and that the Spirit of God dwelleth in you." This is the secret of holiness, to be filled with the Holy Spirit: This is the secret of victory over self and sin: "The spirit lusteth against the flesh; walk in the Spirit and ye shall not fulfil the lusts of the flesh." This is the secret of power: "Ye shall receive the power of the Holy Ghost coming upon you. This is the secret of peace and joy: "The Kingdom of God is righteousness and peace and joy in the Holy Ghost." This is the bond of union and the channel of communion with Jesus: "He shall take of mine and show it unto you." Everything that comes to us from Jesus is dispensed to us by the Holy Ghost. Every true prayer is His inner breath, and every note of praise is His upspringing. O, how we should receive and cherish this Heavenly Guest and give Him the very innermost shrine of the heart's temple.

But the second passage speaks of an indwelling in the body as well as the spirit. "Know you not that your body is the temple of the Holy Ghost?" This is quite distinct and brings a new experience of physical consecration,

89

healing and life. In the verses just before we are told that the body is for the Lord and the Lord for the body and the members are united to Christ in the holiest bonds. And here he tells us that this is made real through the Holy Ghost, who comes into our body and takes possession of it for Christ, bringing the life of Jesus into it, and uniting it to Him in the great mystery of the Body of Christ. This is not the only place the Spirit is spoken of as the life and healer of the body. We read of Samson that all his physical strength was due to the moving of the Holy Ghost upon his frame. And in the eighth chapter of Romans the Spirit is said to "quicken our mortal body" when He dwelleth in us. So here we can understand how this physical possession of the Holy Ghost should be emphasized in distinction from His spiritual indwelling in the previous passage. The old transcribers were evidently afraid of giving undue prominence to the body in this passage, and, with a tinge of the ascetic spirit, they managed to insert the clause in the last verse, "and spirit, which are God's." But the revisers have seen the error and left it out, and the passage stands before us in all its naked simplicity, a glorious plea for our physical salvation through Christ and the Holy Ghost. God is not afraid to give the body its fullest place in the plan of redemption in the work of the Spirit in the body of Christ and for the glory of God. Let us not fear to, but let our body be the glad and consecrated temple of the Holy Ghost, and let Him so live within and shine forth from His own dwelling that we shall GLORIFY GOD IN OUR BODY, WHICH IS GOD'S.

III. – THE SPIRIT IS AN ENDOWMENT FOR SERVICE.

Having taught us the work of the Spirit as our teacher and keeper, the apostle now leads us to consider and understand His great ministry in preparing us for service.

To this subject the whole of the twelfth chapter is devoted. Many important principles are brought out in these profound sentences.

1. The whole church is regarded as the Body of Christ.

2. The body is one, the same in every age, possessing the same Head, the same life, the same union with Christ, the same spirit, the same powers and gifts and ministries. There are not two bodies, the one apostolic and the other modern, but we are in the same body as Paul and John, and the least little finger in all the body has a right to the whole power of the Head and the whole life of the members.

3. Every member of the body is absolutely dependent upon the Holy Ghost for the least ministry; so that no man can even rightly confess Jesus Christ as Lord except by the Holy Ghost. It is not natural talent but spiritual gifts that God uses to serve Him in the church.

4. There are diversities of gifts and ministries, but the same spirit works through all, so that all are equally divine and honorable, the service of giving as sacred as that of preaching, the office of a "help" being as high as that of a "government;" indeed, placed before it in the divine category. All have not therefore the same offices and services, yet each may aim to have the best ministries, and more even than one if they can fill them all to the glory of God.

5. The various ministries and gifts bestowed upon the church for all time include wisdom, knowledge, faith, teaching, the working of miracles, the healing of the sick, the government of the church, and all other service in the work of the Gospel.

6. The power for these ministries is not vested in the person to whom they are entrusted, as a personal power and a gift under their own control, but it is simply the Holy Spirit Himself choosing to work through them and using them only as instruments, who have no glory and no power apart from Him, and can only be used as He

91

pleases and leads. "All these worketh that one and self-same Spirit, dividing to every one severally as He will."

7. To every one is given some ministry, gift and enduement, which the receiver may improve and increase by humble and holy use. "The manifestation of the Spirit is given to every one to profit withal." Like the pounds in the parable of Luke 19, we may so improve the gifts the Spirit bestows that they shall greatly multiply, and we become tenfold useful.

Now, these are some of the principles of Christian service. With such resources and such a source of power none need be useless, idle or feeble. The engine of Infinite Power is within reach. We have but to turn on the power and all God's fulness comes into our weakness and our work. While we are crying: "Awake! awake! O, arm of the Lord," let us rather hear Him saying: "Awake! awake! put on thy strength, O, Zion!" Blessed Holy Spirit, our Teacher, our Indwelling Guest, our wondrous Worker and self-sufficient Power, to Him be honor and glory, everlasting. Amen.

CHAPTER VII.

CHRISTIAN LIFE IN
SECOND CORINTHIANS

"Not that we are sufficient of ourselves, to think anything as of ourselves, but our sufficiency is of God, who also hath made us able ministers of the New Testament. – 2Cor. 3:5.

AN English minister was once travelling in the Highlands of Scotland, and, while dining at a village inn, he spoke to the girl who waited upon him about her soul. Finding her unsaved and indifferent, he asked her to make him one promise, that she would every day repeat these two simple prayers: "Lord, show me myself. Lord, show me Thyself."

She made the promise, and they parted. Many years went by, and one Sabbath morning, at the close of his sermon in his church in London, a gray haired woman came up to him and asked to speak with him. She asked him if he remembered stopping once at a Highland inn and speaking to the girl that waited upon him, long ago, and then she told him how for months she mechanically repeated the promised prayer every night without feeling or expecting any result, and then how troubles came to her, and her own heart got wrong and things grew darker and darker, until, at last, she was in absolute despair. Instead of getting better she seemed to grow worse, until her own heart was a terror to her, and she seemed incapable even of a prayer. Then it suddenly flashed upon her that God had been answering her prayer and revealing, to her her own heart, and then she fell on her knees and cried: "Lord, Thou hast shown me myself, now show me Thyself." And so, day by day, she prayed

93

and looked away to Christ, until there began to rise before her heart the vision of one who had came to be the substitute for her, the answer for her sins, the remedy for her failures, the supply of her needs and the filling up of all her shortcomings and deficiencies. So that the more fully she had seen herself, the more perfectly it enabled her to understand the Saviour's fitness and fulness for her need and nothingness, and now she had come, with the snows of years and the sunlight of heaven on her brow, to thank him for his word of benediction, and to tell him that his little seed by the wayside had borne most blessed fruit.

I.

Let us apply these two principles to the healing of the body. Paul begins this epistle with his physical experience of redemption. In the first chapter he tells us that he had just passed through a violent attack of illness, in which he was "pressed out of measure so that he despaired even of life," and that he had even passed sentence of death upon himself – that is, that he gave up all hope of life through any conditions in himself. But just then, when his own hopes failed and he found all his resources INSUFFICIENT, then he found the Divine resources at hand to lift him up and restore him. Our trust was not in ourselves, he says, "but in God who raiseth the dead, who delivered us from so great a death, who doth still deliver, and in whom we trust that He will yet deliver us."

So again, in the fourth chapter, he tells us that this was his daily physical experience. "We have this treasure," he says, that is the life of Christ, "in earthen vessels, that the excellency of the power might be of God and not of us." And again, "we which live are always delivered unto death for Jesus' sake, that the life also of Jesus might be made manifest in our mortal flesh." That is, the

94

natural life fails – INSUFFICIENT – the life of Christ takes its place, and so "OUR SUFFICIENCY IS OF GOD."

Thus, in Divine Healing, we do not get always a strong body, but a strong Christ for a weak body, and His power is more wondrously displayed in so using and keeping an earthen vessel than if the vessel were made of gold or stone, and free, intrinsically, from frailty and infirmity

II.

Again, this is the principle of mental and spiritual power, life and blessing. "Not sufficient even to think anything as of ourselves," is a pretty severe sentence upon a gifted brain and a trained intellect. It would be a good thing if some other brains could pass the same sentence on themselves, and cease from their own pride and self-confidence. Then God could teach them and Christ reveal Himself to them. Then we should be able soon to add: "Our sufficiency is of God who also hath made us able ministers of the New Testament."

This is also true of the spiritual life. There, too, we must come down to insufficiency before we can find His all-sufficiency. The story of the Bible is largely a story of failure. Adam fails, and with him the whole race, and then the All-sufficient comes in to save. Job breaks down under trial and confesses his self-abhorrence, and then God becomes his vindicator and restorer. Israel completely fails under the old covenant, and then God gives the new covenant and guarantees to keep our hearts as well as His own promises and covenants. "Blessed are the poor in spirit," the Master says to the insufficient ones, "for theirs is the kingdom of Heaven." It is by going down and giving up that we get where we can take Him for all. The measure of our grace is the depth of our conscious need. God has, therefore, to let us fail at every point to see our need of Him, and as each new testing shows a new need, we are ready to receive Christ in

95

some new way and measure. Thus we are led on, step by step, as we are able, and at last we find that there is no place where the Lord Jesus Christ cannot be a perfect substitute for us. All we need is fully to see ourself, and then, over against it, Himself.

III.

The same principle applies to our circumstances. In the twelfth chapter, Paul gives us a section of his experience, and tells us how the circumstances grew too hard for him, and he felt he must have them changed. So three times he asked the Lord to remove the trial. But the Lord answered: "My grace is sufficient for thee, for my strength is made perfect in weakness." That is, let the trial come, let the strength of nature fail to meet it, and then let the grace of Jesus be proved sufficient.

The pearl oyster sometimes receives into its tiny shell a sharp and irritating grain of sand. The most natural thing would be to try to throw it out. But this would only rasp and lacerate its sensitive flesh, and produce pain, disease and death. Instead of this, it throws out an exquisite crystalline fluid, with which it covers and smothers the rude obstruction, and makes it free from all friction and annoyance, until gradually the rough grain of sand grows into a beautiful pearl. So the Lord Jesus can meet the most trying circumstance with His grace and love, and so cover it over with His comfort and blessing that out of it will grow the most precious experience of our existence, and the very jewel and crown of our Christian life.

Shall we take that great Word today without rebate, discount or compromise, "My grace is sufficient for thee," and answer back in victory and faith: "Yes, Thy grace is sufficient for me; I AM INSUFFICIENT, BUT CHRIST IS ALL-SUFFICIENT." Yes, it is ALL-SUFFICIENCY. There is no need, there is no excuse, there must be no provision for failure. When Henry of England sent the Black

Prince, his son, into the battle of Cressy, he stood off on a neighboring height with a large force of reserves, and said: "My son, you must win this battle; but if you feel that you cannot stand longer, signal to me, and all these legions will be at your side." The very thought that his father and all those battalions were there was an inspiration worth twenty thousand men. The sight of yonder floating flag meant all sufficiency, and he fought as he had never fought before, and hastened at nightfall to lay his laurels at his father's feet with a proud and beating heart. So, on yonder heights, He waits, all-sufficient and ever at your call. *He will never fail you.* O, let it nerve you for this conflict and change your wailings to shouts of praise and songs of victory. "Thanks be unto God who giveth us the victory through our Lord Jesus Christ." "Thanks be unto God who always causeth us to triumph in Christ." "The Lord will deliver me from every evil work, and preserve me unto His heavenly kingdom." "God is able to make all grace abound so that we always having all-sufficiency in all things, may abound unto every good work." "We are not sufficient even to think anything as of ourselves, *but our sufficiency is of God.*" In His name we set up our banners. There are two. One trails in the dust: MYSELF – INSUFFICIENT. The other floats aloft: HIMSELF – ALL-SUFFICIENT. To Him be the glory forever and ever, Amen.

CHAPTER VIII

CHRISTIAN LIFE IN GALATIANS
CRUCIFIED WITH CHRIST.

"I am crucified with Christ; nevertheless, I live, yet not I but Christ liveth in me, and the life I now live in the flesh, I live by the faith of the Son of God, who loved me and gave Himself for me." – Gal. 2:16.

I. – CRUCIFIXION.

*T*HE first view which Paul gives us of the Christian life in this precious Epistle is as a life of crucifixion. This does not mean a life of continual crucifixion, but a life of accomplished crucifixion. Much of the point of the Holy Spirit's teaching lies in tenses. And the tense here in the original is most emphatic. "I HAVE BEEN CRUCIFIED with Christ." It is not dying, but death. Many people are always dying or trying to die, but they are not dead, and their life is one of torture and inefficiency. They live out all the agony of a living death, and yet never have the rest of real death. There is no pain in death, it is all in the dying. The Scriptural teaching is of an act of death, definite, final and real. So that we are henceforth to reckon ourselves DEAD INDEED, unto sin.

Now, this is the true secret of Christian life and holiness. It is not the cleansing of the natural heart, but the killing of it. It is not the development of the good in us, but the destruction of our old life and the implanting of a nature wholly new and divine. Its true symbol is baptism, a death and burial of self, outright, and a new and everlasting life in Him. When I was a boy I owned

99

an apple tree; I was very proud of it; I had seen it grow from a little seedling, and I cherished it like a very child. Proudly I watched it as it grew taller and stronger, and from a slender sapling branched out into an ample tree. My brother had one also; but I noticed with triumph that mine was by far the larger, and seemed to look down on his modest little bush. At last the first blossom appeared. O, how I watched it, and mourned when it withered, and waited a whole year for the next promise of fruit. At last the first little, marble shaped apples hung upon the branches. There were only three or four, but they were worth more than gold to me. It seemed that I must watch them from the hungry birds and insects. All the world seemed to be watching for my apples. But the birds let them alone, and it was not long ere I found the reason why. *They were miserable crabs.* Bitterly I tried one after another in vain. They were hard and sour and useless. Year after year I tried to improve my tree, but it was vain. It bore plenty of fruit, but it was all the same, hard, sour, useless crabs. And there beside it was my brother's tree, with its modest form and rich, ripe, mellow fruit, mocking all my boasting and my proud endeavors. What was the difference? Ah! when a little thing his tree had been cut down to the quick and another branch from a fruitful tree had *been grafted on,* and the old tree's life had died and given place to the new. It was the story of self-crucifixion, and God has since taught me in the spiritual life the lesson of my childhood's apple tree. How often have I seen men and women struggling to improve their natural heart by resolves, sacrifices, examples, and all possible human influences, and when all was done it was only the poor carnal heart dressed up a little. God's secret is the death-stroke and the divine engrafting. It is the utter, everlasting putting off the old man as well as his deeds, and counting no more on any natural thing within us for a

100

good thought, or act, or feeling, but depending for all upon the momentary supply of the life of Christ.

Now, this definite, absolute, and final putting off of ourselves in an act of death, is something we cannot do ourselves. It is not self-mortifying, but it is dying with Christ. There is nothing can do it but the Cross of Christ and the Spirit of God. The church is full of half dead people who have been trying like poor Nero, to slay themselves for years, and have not had the courage to strike the fatal blow. O, if they would just put themselves at Jesus' feet, and let Him do it, there would be accomplishment and rest. On that Cross He has provided for our dying as well as our life, and our part is just to let His death be applied to our old nature just as it has been to our old sins, and then leave it with Him, think no more about it, and count it dead, not recognizing it any longer as ourselves, but another, refusing to listen or to fear it, to be identified with it, or even to try to cleanse it, but counting it utterly in His hands and dead to us forever, and for all our new life depending on Him at every breath, as a babe just born depends upon a mother's life.

Crucifixion, therefore, is not so much constantly mortifying the old life as wholly ceasing from it and treating it as if it were not, fearing even the thought and memory of it, and feeling that the touch of it even to wound or kilt it would be as defiling as the touch of a putrid corpse. It is committed to Christ; it is in His hands. We have absolutely *nothing* to do with it but to leave it, and evermore to leave it there.

What becomes of it? The very question is unwholesome. We are not even to pursue it in thought. The Lord knows and the Lord has it in His hands, and we leave it to Him. What if it should struggle in the throes of a lingering death; what if, like the serpent's tail, it should quiver till the sun goes down; what though the grave where it lies should shudder sometimes with its struggle to arise, leave it to Him. Fear not; touch it not; it is no longer you, and it is no longer your care or conflict.

II. – RESURRECTION.

"Nevertheless, I live." There is now a new life. It has descended from above. It is a new creation. It is born out of Christ's very heart. It has no ingredient of the old nature in it. It is as if we had just come down out of heaven, and never lived here before. It is "the heart of flesh," "the new man," "the seed" that remaineth in him that is born of God; the life that is "hid with Christ in God," the mystery of the new birth. Into the flesh of a caterpillar the ichneumon drops an egg with its long and pointed lance-like sting. Warmed by the body of its victim, it hatches and springs to life, and then begins to feed on the caterpillar's flesh. Slowly the caterpillar declines, until it is but a crawling shell. The little ichneumon lives within grows to maturity, and then bursts its shell and goes forth into the fulness of perfect life. So within this encompassing house of clay the Holy Spirit drops the seed of life divine   It seems at times almost hid, but it is imperishable and eternal. It has no more part with the old natural heart than the little ichneumon with the caterpillar. And so it grows to its maturity, and at last will burst even the worn out fetters of clay, and spring into the life immortal above.

III. – CHRIST OUR LIFE.

But this is not all. "Yet not I but CHRIST LIVES IN ME." There is more than a new life born of Christ. Christ Himself comes to live in this new heart, and it is only a little branch in Him, the mighty vine, only a little member, receiving all its vital strength every moment from His great heart of love. So that it has no strength apart from Him, and lives only by abiding in Him and he in it. Not only has it ceased from its old self, of nature
102

and sin, but it now learns daily to cease from the new self and draw its life momentarily from Him. It is ever still, "not I but Christ liveth in me." Does it need grace? "My grace is sufficient for thee." Do we need peace? "My peace I give unto thee." Do we need strength? "Let him take hold of My strength." Do we need anything? "Put on the Lord Jesus." When we cease from our strength He will give His. When we really believe, "apart from Me ye can do nothing," we will learn, "I can do all things through Christ that strengtheneth me."

Nay, so completely are we dependent upon Him for the maintenance of our life that in this verse our very faith is spoken of as if it were not ours but His, "The life I live in the flesh I live BY THE FAITH OF THE SON OF GOD." We are not capable of a single act of effectual faith apart from Him but simply receive of Him and exercise in union with Him the perfect trust which He possesses and inbreathes. He knows no doubt, no fear, no distrust, and filled with Him our heart trusts like His own, and lives by the faith of the Son of God. O, what a remedy for doubt and fear it is to let Jesus reign within.

IV. – A LIFE IN THE SPIRIT.

In the next chapter we are introduced to the part which the Holy Spirit performs in this new life.

First, we receive Him by simple faith. "Received ye the Spirit by the works of the law or by faith?" We did not attain this experience, but yielded ourselves up in helplessness to Him, and then trusted the Holy Spirit just as we trusted Jesus. Many Christians do not trust the Holy Ghost. They will not believe His promises or rest in His abiding Presence without some sign or token, and they are always afraid of Him either deserting them or leading them into something terrific. We must trust Him and rest upon Him. The Rock gives out its waters not by striking it but by speaking to it.

Secondly, He comes as the Spirit of Jesus to shed abroad in our hearts the trust and love of Christ, and bring to us the consciousness of our sonship. "Because ye are sons God hath sent forth the Spirit of His Son into your hearts, crying Abba, Father;" or, as it literally means, in the language of infant simplicity, "Papa, Father."

Thirdly, He comes to fight the battle with the flesh, and overcome sin in you. "The flesh lusteth against the Spirit and the Spirit against the flesh." Now, most of us have supposed that this meant our spirit and our flesh, and they have gone on fighting the flesh till they have become defiled and discouraged by its unhallowed touch and inveterate power. We have nothing to do with it. We have handed it over to Christ, and He gives it in charge to the Holy Spirit who dwells within us to resist and destroy. It is THE SPIRIT, not the spirit that lusteth against the flesh. Our part is simply this: "If ye walk in the Spirit, ye shall not fulfill the lusts of the flesh." We walk in Him and talk with Him and live out His sweet, pure impulses, and He will manage the flesh.

Hercules was asked to clean the Augean stables, where the filth of generations had accumulated. He undertook the task, but, instead of touching the unclean spot with one of his fingers, he simply took a spade and dug a channel for the river to flow through them and in a few minutes they were clean.

God does not want you to wash your own poor heart. You would die of malaria in the attempt. Let the RIVER in and the Holy Ghost will do His own cleansing and keep you clean.

Fourthly, He comes to give and sustain all the positive graces of Christian character and life. "The fruit of the Spirit is love, joy, peace, long suffering gentleness, goodness, faith, meekness, temperance." These are the qualities of Christian character which the Holy Spirit brings. They are not natural virtues, they are "fruit," they

104

grow spontaneously from the Divine life within us. They are not tied on as a Tahitian ties coconuts to the tree that grows over his dead, that he may have food to eat in the spirit world, but they grow up sweetly and freely. There is no effort, no acting a part, but it is second nature, divine nature to do it.

They are, as has been well said, all just so many forms of love, and love is always free. Joy is love exulting, peace is love reposing, long suffering is love enduring, gentleness is love refining, goodness love in action, faith love confiding, meekness love stooping, temperance love restraining itself for the good of others. A heart filled with the Holy Ghost will grow into these, just as a lily watered will grow into white flower cups of fragrance and beauty.

V. – SONSHIP.

This glorious epistle makes it very clear that the ideas which many Christians have of adoption have no place in the Word of God. "Because ye are sons God hath sent forth the Spirit of His Son into our hearts, crying 'Abba, Father,'" or literally "Papa, Father." The word Father is the same in all languages, and is variously expressed by the words "Ba" and "Pa." The idea is that the very simplest name of infant trust is that which God wants us to give Him. He wants to be our "Papa" just as literally as the father on whose strong and faithful breast we have so often leaned our head, and to whose side we have gone so gladly for counsel and help. We are sons, just as He is the Son of God. "My Father and your Father, my God and your God."

VI. – LIBERTY.

The allegory of Hagar and Ishmael is intended to show us the difference between the servile and the filial spirit.

Many Christians are more than half under the law and they have little power, liberty or love. But God says: "Thou art no more a servant, but a son." "Stand fast in the liberty wherewith Christ has made you free, and be not entangled again with the yoke of bondage." We are not free in any sense which would give us liberty to obey the old nature. This would be bondage. "Use not your liberty as an occasion to the flesh." You are free in the new life to love and serve God and your neighbor in all the glorious instincts and impulses of the life of God.

VII. – LOVE.

This is the crowning jewel of this cluster of precious things. Love that "worketh no ill to his neighbor;" love that is ready to "serve one another;" love, the queen of all the graces, with joy, peace, gentleness, long suffering, as sweet sisters, are following by her side; love that restores the erring one in the spirit of meekness; love bearing one another's burdens, and so fulfilling the law of Christ, this is the consummation, this is the spiritual crown, the greatest of all is charity.

In the beautiful Epistle to the Colossians, after describing the dress of the believer, the kindness, the humbleness, the meekness, the forbearance, he adds, as the crowning robe: "Above all these, put on charity," or love, which is the bond of perfectness, literally, the perfect girdle. Without this, all experiences, all baptisms of blessing, all works are vain. After enumerating the deepest experiences of the Holy Spirit in First Corinthians, and all the highest gifts of power, he adds that final chapter about love, in which he tells us that higher and greater than all these is the grace of love, and that without it the sufferings of a martyr, the gifts of a Barnabas, or the eloquence of an Apollos are worth no more than the empty sounds of a tinkling cymbal. If Christ be in us, if we be deeply spiritual, if the heart is

106

the temple of God, we shall be filled with love, "for God is love, and he that dwelleth in love dwelleth in God and God in Him."

CHAPTER IX.

CHRISTIAN LIFE IN EPHESIANS; OR, LIFE IN HEAVENLY PLACES.

"Blessed be the God and Father of our Lord Jesus Christ, who hath blessed us with all spiritual blessings in Heavenly places in Christ." – Eph. 1:3

---

*T*HIS expression, "on heavenly places," occurs often enough in the Epistle to the Ephesians, to give character to the whole letter. It is, indeed, a picture of Christian life on its very highest plane, rising step by step to the very throne of the ascended Christ, where the apostle contemplates it at last, as seated with Him in victorious exaltation.

I.

It begins, as in the other Epistles, *with the initial step of faith.* Ye "first trusted in Christ." This trust is founded on "the Gospel of your salvation," and it is the simple faith which justifies and saves every believer in Jesus.

II.

The next stage is *"sealed with the Holy Spirit of Promise."* This is the personal reception of the Holy Ghost into the heart in such a way as to be definite and unmistakable, like the seal upon the wax, leaving the image of Christ, and putting the stamp of God's ownership, possession, and indwelling upon the soul, and giving to it the security of His presence

III.

Then follows the special *illuminating and anointing of the Spirit,* who has now taken possession, to reveal Jesus in a deeper relationship to the soul; "the Spirit of wisdom and revelation in the knowledge of Him; the eyes of your understanding being enlightened, that ye may know what is the hope of His calling, and what is the riches of the glory of His inheritance in the saints."

IV.

This brings us into a nearer and closer relationship with Christ *in His resurrection and ascension.* Up to this time we have chiefly known Him as the Crucified, but now we see Him as the Risen One, alive for evermore for us, exalted above all power as our Living Head, and pledging to us, in His very resurrection grace and power equal to the exceeding greatness of the power that raised Him from the dead and set Him at His own right hand.

And not only do we see Him as alive, but also as ascended and seated in victory and glory at the right hand of God, and we are seated with Him in the heavenly places, resting in and sharing all His enthroned power. Three great stages have to be passed before we come thus far – crucifixion, resurrection, ascension. Thus to know Jesus lifts us above all the clouds and discouragements of this life, and being's rest and victory.

V.

But there is a still deeper experience. He brings it in the last paragraph of the third chapter. It is to know the fulness of the *indwelling Christ.* In order to know this, we need to be "strengthened with might by the Spirit in the inner man." The natural heart cannot know or receive this "mystery which has been hid from ages and

110

generations, but is now made manifest in His saints, which is Christ in you – the hope of glory." Five things are said of this experience. First, the Spirit prepares us for it; secondly, faith receives it, or rather receives Him for it. Thirdly, love perfects it, and enables us to know the measureless heights and depths of His love. Fourthly, it brings into our life "all the fulness of God." And finally it leads us to the infinities of the Christian life, and opens to faith the treasures of grace which are "exceeding abundant above all that we are able to ask or think."

VI.

The apostle next unfolds to us the Christian life *in its collective capacity in the Body of Christ.* This is the glorious theme of the fourth chapter. Beginning in the individual it is completed and perfected in the unity of the Church of Christ. He presents it under the two figures of a building and a body, showing the mutual dependence of each member and the common life of the whole in the unity of the Spirit, the one Lord, one faith, one baptism, one God and Father of all, who is above all and through all and in your all. This glorious body is growing up through the ages into all its parts, and its full maturity and completeness. To it are given the various gifts and ministries of the Spirit, and at length it will "come to the measure of the stature of the fulness of Christ," and receiving the head-stone in the new Jerusalem, become the eternal monument of redemption, and the wonder and admiration of eternal ages.

VII.

A sudden transition now passes over the Epistle, and it descends from the sublime heights of spiritual elevation to *the practical duties of Christian life.* It is very solemn and suggestive that the Epistle, which gives us our very

111

highest conceptions of lofty spiritual attainment, gives us also the most explicit and detailed directions about every day morality and common place duty and practical righteousness. Those who are risen with Christ, seated with Him in heavenly places and filled with all the fulness of God, are warned against stealing, lying, strife, uncleanness, drunkenness and dishonesty, and called to walk in love, purity and practical holiness in all the secular, social and domestic relations of life. This glorious Christ comes not to sit upon an isolated throne, but to walk in us through the same trials and temptations which once before encompassed His own paths. This celestial robe is not given for the heavenly banquet, but for the mortal strife, to warm us and to cover us in the rough contact of an evil world, and to shine unspotted amid the smoke and dust and filth of our daily walk. There is no situation where we may not and must not live the life of faith and holiness, and find Christ in us sufficient for the kitchen and the counting-room as He is for the closet and the clerical desk. And the neglect of these common things will nullify all our spiritual claims and prove a fatal snare in the path of holiness. Many a man or woman begins such a life all right, and stumbles, not over the theory of Christ's abiding presence, or even the experience of it, but over some little straw in his path in the form of a trifling disobedience, a little temptation to anger or strife, or unrighteousness, but just as fatal as if it were a mountain instead of a straw. To live a higher Christian life,

> "We need not bid for cloistered cell,
> Our neighbor and our work farewell,
> Or seek to wind ourselves too high
> For mortal man beneath the sky.
> The daily round, the common task,
> Will furnish all we need to ask.
> Room to deny ourselves a road
> To bring us daily nearer God."

112

A man in London bought a cheap umbrella, and afterwards brought it back to the maker, complaining that it had gone to pieces. The man looked at it and then, turning to the purchaser, gravely raised his spectacles and said, "You must have been taking it out and getting it wetted." The religion of Jesus is not for fine weather and sweet seclusion. It will stand wetting. And if it won't, we don't want it.

VIII.

The last picture of this great Epistle is *conflict and victory*. Not only in the practical duties of life must our armor be tested, but in the very thick of the fight, and in the conflict with the very principalities and powers of hell. When his armorer had made a breastplate for Napoleon, he made the man put it on while he fired at him. The man got frightened, and Napoleon refused the armor. God's panoply is not for mere parades, but for practical warfare. Indeed, the Epistle teaches us that the nearer we get to heaven, and the higher the elevation of our Christian life, the more bitter and persistent will be the resistance and defiance of hell. The wild waves of evil roll right up to the breakwater of the harbor, and the conflict oft heightens as it nears the close. And there is sometimes the "evil day," when it seems as if all the hosts of hell had combined their forces to crush us by a combined attack. But the armor of God is enough for this too. The provisions of grace are sufficient not only to "withstand but to quench all the fiery darts of the devil." There is armor for the loins, the mighty and eternal truth and faithfulness of God; there is armor for the breast, even the spotless and perfect righteousness of Christ, not only on us but in our breast; there is armor for our feet – namely, the blessed ministry of winning souls through the Gospel of peace, and they, whose feet are thus occupied, will be saved from a thousand occasions

113

of temptation, and will escape a defensive by pursuing an aggressive war. There is armor for the head, where so many get fatally wounded by all they know and think – the simple helmet of God's salvation and its blessed assurance. There is armor for our aggressive war in the sword of the Spirit, which is the word of God before whose thrusts the devil cannot stand. And outside of and covering all is the shield of faith, which meets and repels all the devil's fiery darts, and keeps us so completely covered that "that wicked one toucheth us not." Finally, there is the mighty weapon of prayer, in which the Holy Spirit is ever leading us out, if He dwells within us, and thus meeting as quickly as it comes every need of the soul; and not only so, but even much more carrying war into the enemy's country, and making bold and mighty assaults upon his strongholds and subjects.

Yes, Christ is sufficient for temptation. It is a hard and bitter strife, and sometimes in the evil day it looks almost as if we must sink. But "thanks be to God, who giveth us the victory through our Lord Jesus Christ," we shall "withstand," and "having done all we shall stand." But only those who know Christ thus can stand. Only those who have entered into His risen and ascended life, and received Him in His fulness and been sealed by His Spirit, can meet these awful tests.

Indeed, the average Christian, living in self and sin, knows nothing of them. Yielding easily to the suggestions of Satan, he never knows the pressure of resistance. And Satan need not waste on him the batteries of his power. He is his already. Such a life is full of darkness. But he that overcometh shall inherit all things. And in the crowning day he shall not regret one conflict and tear, as he cries, "Nay, in all these things we are more than conquerors through Him that loved us," and then lays the crown of victory at Jesus' feet.

Beloved, are we armed for this battle? We have not to make the weapons, but only to put them on. They are

114

already made. The truth, the righteousness, the faith, are not ours but His. Our part is simply to take them, wear them, use them, and prove them. It is not our might, but His might. "Finally, then, my brethren, be strong in the Lord, and in the power of His might. Put on the whole armor of God that ye may be able to stand against the wiles of the devil; therefore, take unto you the whole armor of God that ye may be able to withstand in the evil day, and having done all to stand."

CHAPTER X.

CHRISTIAN LIFE IN PHILIPPIANS
THE CHRISTIAN TEMPER

"Let this mind be in you which was also in Christ Jesus." – Phil. 2:5.

---

*T*HE TEMPER of a tool is of much more importance than its size or exquisite finish. So in character there is a fine and subtle quality that consists not so much in any one element or disposition as in the combination of all, and the spirit that underlies the whole, giving flavor and coloring to the whole character. It is this which the Epistle to the Philippians especially depicts in its beautiful portraiture of the Christian life.

I.

He first shows us the Christian temper as it appears in Christ. Two elements underlie it all, viz.: Self-renunciation to the extent of crucifixion, and secondly, Resurrection and exaltation.

Our Lord's descent began at yonder throne, and His ascension takes Him back to a still higher throne. But, like Joseph's, it is still a throne of self-forgetting love, much more, even, than Divine Majesty.

First, He did not try to grasp even his Divine rights, and His own primeval glory. He was in the form of God and equal with God. And yet He counted it not a thing to be grasped or clung to. What a lesson for the spirit of self-seeking, the men and women that are contending for their rights, the people that are standing for their place and dignity and interest. The whole system of the papacy

117

began in the question of precedence among the Archbishops of Rome, Constantinople, Antioch, Jerusalem and Alexandria, as to who should sit next the Emperor at dinner and walk first in the state processions. The Master leading the procession of humiliation, the Church walking in the front rank of earthly pride! Well might the noble Savonarola contrast the pomp of ecclesiastical splendor in his day with the pictures on their cathedral walls of the lowly Galilean walking among the fishermen Apostles or riding on the foal of an ass, and refuse the red hat of a cardinal that He might wear the crimson badge of martyrdom.

He made Himself of no reputation. The world values reputation, that is, the estimate which others have of us. It is one of the dearest forms of self-life and one of the hardest to let go. Christ gave it all up. This does not mean that He gave up that which lies back of reputation, viz., character, purity and truth, but He gave up men's estimate of Him, and chose a path which He knew they would misunderstand and misrepresent He was content to wait for His reputation when the ages should know His grace and love. I have heard of a man in Italy living in great meanness and poverty all his days, although supposed to very rich, and so accused of the basest stinginess, and treated as one that grudged even his humble villagers the wages for which he might have employed them, and then, at his death, receiving scarcely the burial of a pauper; but afterwards it was found that he had economized so closely for the purpose of leaving his whole accumulated estate to those very villagers, with the view of building waterworks and other improvements for the wretched town. They gave him back his reputation when it was too late. But he gladly gave it up for love's sake. So Christ literally became disreputable and was counted by the religious people of His day a devil and a deceiver, and at last treated as a malefactor and a villain, for love of us. How much of your social

118

influence, your ministerial reputation, your standing in the world have you sacrificed for Jesus Christ?

One of the hardest things for a lofty and superior nature is to be under authority to renounce his own will, and to take a place of subjection. But Christ took upon Him the form of *a servant*, gave up His independence, His right to please Himself, His liberty of choice, and after having from eternal ages known only to command gave Himself up only to obey. I have seen occasionally the man who was once a wealthy employer a clerk in the same store. It was not an easy or a graceful position, I assure you. But Jesus was such a perfect servant that His Father said: "Behold my servant, in whom my soul delighteth." All His life His watchword was: The Son of Man came to minister; I am among you as He that doth serve; I can do nothing of myself. Not my will but Thine be done. Have you, beloved, learned the servant's place?

And, once more, "He became obedient unto death, ever the death of the cross." His life was all a dying, and at last He gave all up to death, and also shame, the death of crucifixion lingering, disgraceful, and unspeakably painful. This was the consummation of His love. This was to be the secret of His life and victory and great salvation. "Except a corn of wheat fall into the ground and die," He had said of His own life, "it abideth alone, but if it die, it bringeth forth much fruit." And it is just as true of us. "He that loveth his life shall lose it, but he that hateth his life in this world shall keep it unto life eternal."

There never can be any real sweetness in our Christian temper until we die to ourselves and cease from our own proud will. It is over its grave that all the flowers and fruits of the new life must grow. On the Red Sea an American traveler was burning with fever. He sent out an Arab attendant and asked him to bring him any green thing they could find. They came back late at night with a cactus-like plant, the only green thing that grew in the

119

desert. It seemed strange that such a succulent thing could grow in that soil. But the secret was this: It drew its life from the air, and when its leaves were broken they poured out a crystal water which the traveler could drink with refreshment and delight. Even so our lives must be broken to give forth their sweetness, and therefore it has often been observed that the sweetest spirits are those who have suffered most.

But our Saviour's life was not all humiliation and death. There was also a "resurrection and ascension." "God hath highly exalted Him and given Him a name that is above every Name." And the ascension was as high as the descent had been profound. Indeed, it as far transcends it as eternity transcends a moment. He died once; He is alive forevermore. Thirty-three years He trod the path of humiliation. Eternal ages will but add to the glory of His exaltation. So we, too, share His life as well as His death. There are three stages which we should know, resurrection life, ascension life, millennial life. We are risen with Him, we are seated with Him on His heavenly throne, we shall reign with Him on the earth. Now, Christ never lost sight of His exaltation. It was for the joy set before Him that He endured the cross, despising the shame. And the prospect of that joy made the suffering light and easy. We, too, must keep our eye on the morning. It is this that gives the Christian temper its sweetness and victory. We know we have something better. And we can say, like Cyprian, when they threatened him with the loss of property, friends and life, "You cannot take away my possessions, for my treasure is in heaven; you cannot send me into exile, for Christ will go with me everywhere; you cannot take my life, for my life is hid with Christ in God." It was this that enabled Christ to stoop." "Knowing that He was come from God and went to God," He washed the disciples' feet. The traveler on his way to his elegant home can put up with inconveniences by the way. And if we kept in view our high calling and heavenly inheritance, we would think very little of the trifling annoyances of this life.

Christ, then, is the great type of character. And to have the right temper and character we must have Christ in us. Not the imitation of Christ, but "the SAME mind that was also in Christ Jesus," the Christ Himself living in us, and so imitating Himself in our lives.

II.

Having looked at the great Pattern and Source, the Apostle next proceeds to show the Christian temper as it should be manifested in us. He first gives us some examples of it, and then some characteristics. His own example is the first: "Yea, and if I be offered up on the sacrifice and service of your faith, I joy and rejoice with you all. It is the same spirit of self-sacrifice that we have already seen in Christ.

Next he tells us of Timothy; "I have no man like minded who will naturally care for your state, for all seek their own, not the things that are Christ's, but ye know the proof of him." It is the same unselfishness still.

Then he give us the sweet picture of Epaphroditus, sick nigh unto death, and not regarding his own life to supply their lack of service, and in great heaviness, not on account of his own suffering, but lest it might discourage and hinder them. It is still "the same mind that was also in Christ Jesus," not looking on its own things, but also on the things of others.

He next gives us some of the characteristics of the Christian temper:

1. It springs from a new life. It is not the old natural Pharisaism of Paul or any one else, but a counting all the past, the good as well as the bad, but loss, for the excellency of the knowledge of Christ Jesus our Lord,

and a putting on of His righteousness and the power of His resurrection.

2. It is a life of intense energy and holy aspiration. It counts not itself to have attained, and is not satisfied with any past or present state, but, forgetting "the things which are behind and reaching forth unto those things which are before, it presses toward the mark for the prize of the high calling of God in Christ Jesus our Lord." There is no apathy, no easy self-complacency in it, but intense aspiration, exertion to rise to all for which Christ has called and apprehended us.

3. It is a heavenly-minded temper, separating its possessor from the world and lifting his spirit and his hopes to the spiritual world. "Our conversation is in heaven, from whence we expect also the Saviour the Lord Jesus Christ, who change the body of our humiliation that it may be fashioned like unto the body of His glory, according to the working whereby He is able even to subdue all things unto Himself."

4. It is a loving temper. How tender and affectionate the spirit of this whole epistle. Hear the Apostle as he writes to his Philippian friends: "I have you in my heart, inasmuch as both in my bonds and in the defense and confirmation of the Gospel, ye are all partakers of my grace. For God is my record how greatly I long after you all in the bowels of Jesus Christ."

See how tenderly he speaks of our "consolation in Christ, comfort of love, fellowship of the Spirit, bowels and mercies." Observe how lovingly he pleads with Euodias and Syntyche to be of the same mind in the Lord. Notice how thoughtfully his Philippian converts had provided for his temporal wants, and how tenderly he appreciates and acknowledges it. It seems like the letter of a mother to her children, so full of simple whole-hearted love and its reciprocation. So our Christian life must have the aroma and fragrance of the heart, or it lacks the very fineness of quality which constitutes the home life of God's dear family.

5. It is a joyous temper. Again and again comes the cry: "Rejoice in the Lord." And as a deep undercurrent it runs through the whole letter. It is all written in a tone of triumph. "The things that were against me have turned out to the furtherance of the Gospel." "What I shall choose I wot not" "In nothing terrified by your adversaries." "I count all things but dung that I may win Christ." "If I be offered in sacrifice for you, I joy and rejoice with you all." And so all through, the notes are all of victory and gladness, independent of all circumstances and conditions.

6. It is a peaceful temper. Now, peace is more than even joy, for it is the staple and enduring grace which, like the air we breathe, blends with every part of our life. And the Epistle to the Philippians speaks of a peace which passeth all understanding, a peace which keeps the heart from every care a peace which keeps the mind from every distracting thought, a peace which is nothing less than the very peace of God Himself dwelling in the heart and holding it in His own everlasting rest.

7. It is an even and uniform temper. The great study of mechanical art has been to provide against the expansion and contraction of metals. Even the famous Brooklyn bridge contracts nearly two feet in the entire length in the extremes of a single year's temperature. Provision has to be made for this in the structure of the arches. In the natural life we are affected by every change of circumstances. The spirit that was genial and amiable in the midst of luxury, chafes and frets and grows morbid and malignant in poverty and sorrow. Only the grace of God can make us independent of summer or winter weather in the soul, singing when the blossoms fade from the fig tree as well as amid the sunshine. Such is the spirit of this epistle. "I have learned" – oh, it had to be learned – "in every state I am,

123

therewith to be content." "I know how to be abased and I know how to abound. Everywhere and in all things I am instructed both to be full and to be hungry, both to abound and to suffer need." Such a spirit is independent of all conditions, and can sing:

> "To me remains nor place nor time,
> My country is in every clime,
> And regions none remote I call,
> Secure of finding God in all."

8. The Christian temper is characterized by practical righteousness. A beautiful cluster of Christian graces hangs like a chain of precious jewels about its neck. They are in two groups. One consists of the things that are the essential and fundamental qualities of character. They are classed under the general term, "if there be any virtue," and consist of "whatsoever things are true, whatsoever things are pure, whatsoever things are honest, whatsoever things are just." The other is made up of "whatsoever things are lovely, and whatsoever things are of good report," and is described by the general phrase, "if there be any praise." The first includes the sterling and essential qualities of character; the second, the ornamental. Both are necessary, although the former are the more indispensable. The one is like the solid mountain, the other like the moss-covered sides and cloud dome that surmounts them. The one is like the show bread in the ancient tabernacle, the other the frankincense that covered it. Some men have only got the sterling qualities. They are good and true, but not attractive. God wants the sweetness as well as the strength, the loveliness in the midst of the mightyness, the Lamb in the midst of the throne, the corn but also the wine and the smell of Lebanon.

9. Finally, all this must come from Christ, and Christ is sufficient for it all. "I have learned the secret," the

124

apostle exclaims; "I can do all things through Christ that strengtheneth me." And then, commending to them the same all-sufficient One in believing prayer, he adds: "My God shall supply all your need, according to his riches in glory by Christ Jesus."

Such is the Christian temper as portrayed in this affectionate letter. May the Holy Spirit sweetly transfer it into all our hearts and lives. Or, rather, may we all receive not it, but Him who is not only its Pattern, but also its Living Source; and so "let this mind be in us which was also in Christ Jesus." Amen.

COLOSSE

CHAPTER XI.

CHRISTIAN LIFE IN COLOSSIANS; OR, CHRIST ALL AND IN ALL.

"Christ is all and in all." – Col. 3:11.

*T*HE preeminent purpose of this letter is to exalt the personal glory of Christ. Therefore it is very dear to every devout friend of the Lord Jesus. It was written chiefly to correct certain teachings and tendencies which were creeping into the Church from the philosophizing parties, Jews and Alexandrians, that had already begun to spring up in the early Church, leading ambitious minds away from the simplicity which is in Jesus Christ to novel speculations, "vainly intruding into the things which they had not seen, puffed up with their fleshy mind, and not holding the Head," introducing forms and ceremonies, and professing to unfold the subtle mysteries of some deeper knowledge.

In contrast with all this, Paul fixes their eyes upon Jesus as the substance of all these rites and shadows, and the source of all fulness and blessing.

I. – ALL THE FULNESS OF THE GODHEAD.

Christ is to us the complete embodiment of all there is in God. He expresses to us the purpose and design of God for man. His very mission is a revelation of God's love, and His glorious person is an incarnation of God. In Him the Father is perfectly revealed. "He that hath seen Me hath seen the Father." In Him the Deity of the Son is united. "The life was manifested, and we have seen it, and declare unto you that eternal life which was

127

with the Father and was manifested unto you." "The Word was made flesh and He dwelt among us, and we beheld His glory, even the glory of the duly Begotten of the Father, full of grace and truth." And He was the very temple of the Holy Ghost, who abode upon Him, and is imported from His own very hands. In His person the whole Deity meets us, poor sinful men. Would you know the character of God? Look at Jesus. Would you receive the presence of God? Receive Jesus. Would you be united with the very being of God? Abide in Jesus. Would you be filled with all the fulness of God? Let "Christ dwell in your heart by faith." "No man hath seen God at any time. The only Begotten Son, who is in the bosom of the Father, He hath declared Him." And like the ancient Tabernacle where God and the people met in Him the Father dwells, and in Him the redeemed sinner dwells, and thus divinely reconciled they are one forever.

II. – CHRIST IS THE ALL IN ALL OF CREATION.

"For by Him were all things made that are in Heaven and that are on earth, whether they be thrones or principalities or powers, all things were made by Him and for Him." The whole creation is His work, and made to reveal Him. The natural was made to show forth the spiritual. The world is a microcosm of God. The sun in the Heavens speaks of the Son of Righteousness. The stars that herald the dawn are harbingers of the bright and Morning Star. The light points with its quivering rays to Heaven and cries. "He is the Light of the World." The bread we eat is but a symbol of Him who is the Living Bread, and its buried seed and bruised corn and burning oven all tell how He became for us the life of our life. We drink from the spring, and, lo! a voice whispers, "that rock was Christ." We sit in the circle of home and loved ones, and every tender tie whispers

"Jesus, my husband, brother, friend."

128

In a German village there is a drinking fountain, where as the farmers, shepherds, gardeners, soldiers, children pass by they can see each a marble spout, emblematic of his calling and a Scripture motto above it, connecting it with some aspect of the Saviour. The shepherd came and drank from the fountain where stood the Good Shepherd, cut in marble, holding in His hands a tender lamb. The husbandman drank from the marble amid the familiar forms of vines and clusters of grapes, and read over the crystal waters, "I am the True Vine, abide in Me." The soldier saw a shield with the reminder of the shield of faith. The little child held up its tiny vessel to catch the water, and it flowed from the extended hand of Jesus saying, "Suffer the little children to come unto Me, and forbid them not, for of such is the kingdom of Heaven." So every aspect of nature, and every calling of life, became a type of Christ, and ministered His glory. Should it not be so in all our life. Is it not the song of Heaven about Him. "The whole earth is full of His glory." "All for Him, and all by Him." And it is well to remember that our Jesus is the Creator. When He gives us His greatest promises He reminds us that He is able to make their fulfillment out of nothing. Thus saith the Lord THE MAKER thereof, "Call unto Me and I will answer thee, and show thee great and mighty things that thou knowest not." Why should we doubt His power to help us when we look up into these Heavens and remember that He made them all. He made old Abraham look at the stars, when He was about to give him His greatest promises. O! yes;

> "His word of grace is strong
> As that which built the skies.
> The voice that rolls the stars along
> Spake all the promises."

III. – CHRIST IS ALL IN ALL IN PROVIDENCE.

By Him all things consist or hang together. The system of nature is not a mechanical automaton, running itself, but the intense and ceaseless working of an ever present God. "In Him we live and move and have our being." And that every living moving presence is Jesus Christ. "He was in the world, and the world was made by Him, and the world knew Him not." His intervention and prospective atonement saved the world from immediate judgment and destruction. His redemption has secured to us all our earthly blessings and mercies. His wisdom and love direct the whole course of our lives. On His shoulders rests the government of all our interests. The Lamb is in the midst of the throne. The seals are all opened by His hand. To His gentle ordering belong all the issues on which our longing hearts hang with hope and expectation.

> "Our times are in His hand –
> Jesus the Crucified.
> The hand our many sins have pierced
> Is now our guard and guide.

> "Our times are in His hand,
> Why should we doubt or fear.
> A Saviour's hand will never cause
> His child a needless tear.

IV. – CHRIST IS ALL AND IN ALL IN OUR REDEMPTION.

"Having made peace by the blood of His cross, by Him to reconcile all things to Himself, and you, hath He reconciled in the body of His flesh through death, to present you holy and unblameable and unreprovable in His sight." "In whom we have redemption through His blood, even the forgiveness of sins." "Ye are complete in Him, buried with Him in baptism, wherein ye are also risen with Him, through the faith of the operation of God, who raised Him from the dead. And you being dead in your sins, and the uncircumcision of your flesh, doth He quickened together with Him, having forgiven you all trespasses, blotting out the handwriting of consequences that was against us, and took it out of the way, nailing it to His cross." Thus has He, and He alone, redeemed us fully forever. It is finished. It is final. It is steadfast as His eternal throne. It is His work alone. And to Him be all the glory. The atonement is made. The peace is made. The reconciliation is complete. The handwriting that was against us is blotted out and cancelled, and, then like a paid-up check, that is placed on the file, it is nailed to His cross. Nay, the very devil that defied us has been forever conquered and openly disgraced, and is now hung up like an old scarecrow on the cross of Jesus, that we may never fear him again. Blessed salvation, glorious Saviour, unto Him that loved us, and washed us from our sins in His own blood, be glory and dominion forever and ever. Amen.

V. – CHRIST IS ALL AND IN ALL IN THE TYPES AND SHADOWS OF JUDAISM, AND THE ORDINANCES AND CEREMONIES OF CHRISTIANITY.

"Which were all a shadow of things to come, but the body is Christ." They were in great danger of being led back into the bondage of Jewish ritualism. "Touch not, taste not, handle not." But He teaches them that all these things have found their fulfillment in Christ Himself. And even the abiding ordinances of the New Testament are only drinking vessels, which are vain if they are not filled by Christ out of the living waters of His Spirit and His presence. Baptism is the hardest and deadest ritualism, the Lord's Supper – an empty form, confirmation and ordination, and the very ministry of the Gospel itself, as a sounding brass and tinkling cymbal. All these are only cups, but He is the water and the wine of life, which fills the vessel and satisfies the hungry soul. A service of silver with an empty table would be a poor dinner. And many a splendid church has royal plate and pauper's fare.

VI. – CHRIST IS ALL AND IN ALL IN THE WORLD OF TRUTH AND KNOWLEDGE, AND THE WORD OF GOD.

"In Him are hid all the treasures of wisdom and knowledge." They were in great danger of being led away into the new and fascinating errors of Gnosticism, which just meant knowledge. False and plausible teachers were leading them aside after the speculations of Jewish and heathen philosophy, and the mysteries of forbidden knowledge. And He tells them that Christ holds the key of all true knowledge; nay, is the sum and substance of all truth Himself. The Bible is a portraiture of Jesus, and all we need to know of God is in the Living Word, and it is a great thing when the soul gets beyond ideas, theories, doctrines, feelings, revelations, and rests in Him. "This is eternal life to know Thee and Jesus Christ, whom Thou sent."

> "Christ to trust and Christ to know,
> Constitute our bliss below.
> Christ to see and Christ to love,
> Constitute our bliss above.

VII. – CHRIST IS THE ALL IN ALL OF OUR SPIRITUAL LIFE.

"Ye are complete in Him who is the head of all principality and power. Ye are dead, and your life is hid

132

with Christ in God. If ye then be risen with Christ, seek those things that are above, where Christ sitteth on the right hand of God."

It is not a slowly acquired state, a character built up, a series of virtues gradually attained. It is Christ in us, our complete life. This is the great secret, "the mystery that has been hid from ages and from generations, but is now made manifest to his saints, which is CHRIST IN YOU, THE HOPE OF GLORY." This is the very core of spiritual life. It is not a subjective state so much as a divine person received to abide and rule in the heart. Christ for us is the source of our justification. Christ in us of our sanctification. When this becomes real, "ye are dead," your own condition, states and resources are no longer counted upon any more than a dead man's, but "your life is hid with Christ in God." It is not even always manifest to you. It is hid and so wrapped up and enfolded in Him that only as you abide in Him does it appear and abide. Nay, "Christ, who is your life," must Himself ever maintain it, and be made unto you of God all you need. Therefore, Christian life is not to come to Christ to save you, and then go on and work out your sanctification yourself, but, "as ye have received Christ Jesus the Lord, so to walk in Him, just as dependent and as simply trusting as for your pardon and salvation. And so the successive stages are all as personal. "Rooted and grounded in Him." "Built up in Him." "Complete in Him." "And have put on the new man, where Christ is all and all." Blessed simplicity of life and rest, only to abide in Him, and find Him all we need – peace, purity, power and victory, moment by moment.

VIII. – CHRIST IS ALL AND IN ALL IN OUR OUTWARD LIFE.

"Whatsoever ye do in word or deed do all in the name of the Lord Jesus. Whatsoever ye do, do it heartily as to

133

the Lord and not unto men." That is in all the words and actions of our life let us act just as if it was the Lord Jesus Himself, for that is really the meaning of the phrase, "in His name," that is in His very character and personality; and then, having taken this attitude, expect Him to stand by us, and sustain and carry us through it. We can thus represent Christ in our business, in our household, in our public and private ministries, in our social relationships, in our conversations, in our pleasures, in our trials, so act that people will truly say, as one said of a dear child of God, "I never meet him but I am reminded of the Lord Jesus Christ." Every act in such a life will be sacramental, and over every door His footsteps enter will be this inscription, "Do this in remembrance of Me." Over such a life will hover, evermore, that nameless, viewless, and yet unmistakable presence, which will make men think of God, and seem to bring the Heavenly world so near that there is but a vail between! So we may and should ever walk with the holy majesty of men and women who remember, "I am representing Jesus here, and He is representing me there." My name is written yonder on His breastplate, and His is reflected here in my life. Let us grow less, let Him increase. In old European cities you always find the market under a great wooden cross. O! that all our business were done under the shadow of the cross. So let us lift up Jesus, and make every market place, and every spot we touch a sacramental emblem of our Lord.

IX. – CHRIST IS THE ALL IN ALL OF OUR FUTURE HOPES.

"When Christ, who is our life, shall appear then shall we also appear with Him in glory." This glorious Christ is coming in His kingdom, and going to bring our crowns and our inheritance. The world is looking forward for its golden age, when culture, civilization and liberty shall
134

have covered the earth. The Christian's future is all bound up with the appearing of our Lord. He is not looking for perfect government, social reform, or even the world's conversion, apart from the personal return, and omnipotent reign of its rightful Master and Lord. And for this He is waiting, working, praying and preparing. It is "the blessed hope." It will bring a regenerated world, a resurrection, life, a restitution of all we have lost, and, above all besides, our Lord Himself. For in this too Christ is to be all and In all. He is to be the dear personal object of our desire, and source of our supreme and eternal joy.

> "The bride eyes not her garments,
>   But her dear bridegroom's face.
> I will not gaze at glory,
>   But on the King of Grace,
> Not on the crown He giveth,
>   But on His pierced hand.
> The Lamb is all the glory
>   In Immanuel's land.

X. – CHRIST IS ALL IN ALL IN HIS CHURCH.

"The Head from whom the whole body, by joints and bands having nourishment, ministered and knit together, increaseth with the increase of God." O, that we were, indeed so in the Church of God! O, that this living fellowship were better understood! O, that men and methods and mere ideas might make room for the Master Himself! And in her name and her testimony, her separation from the world, and her devoted love to Him alone, the Church were, indeed, the bride – the Lamb's wife," and on her brow this jeweled memorial shining like a band of burning stars. "Christ is all and in all."

135

CHRISTIAN LIFE IN THESSALONIANS; OR, ENTIRE SANCTIFICATION AS A PREPARATION FOR THE LORD'S COMING.

"The very God of Peace sanctify you wholly; and I pray God your whole spirit and soul and body be preserved blameless unto the coming of our Lord Jesus Christ. Faithful is he that calleth you, who also will do it." – 1Thess. 5:23-24

*T*HE epistles to the Thesselonians are pre-eminently epistles of our Lord's Second Coming. They reveal to us with more fulness than any other of Paul's writings, the details of that glorious hope of the church of God as it affects the church and the world. And then they tell us of the preparation we need to meet Him, the marriage robes of Divine Holiness.

I.

Let us first look at the NECESSITY OF SANCTIFICATION. "This is the will of God, even your sanctification." That leaves no doubt of the way God feels and thinks about our holiness. A great many people think of this matter a good deal as we students used to think about what we called options in the great universities. These were studies which we might or might not take, as we pleased. A certain degree of scholarship was essential to pass the examinations at all. But certain subjects were open, and only those who wished to compete for special prizes took them. So a great many people think that a holy heart and life are things left to our own choice as a sort of competition for a special prize. But God has said "that without holiness no man shall see the Lord." It is the regulation standard of His Kingdom. He commands it. He exemplifies it Himself. He provides it for us. He wills it for us. And you cannot be destitute of it without being contrary to His pure and holy will.

II.

Next consider THE NATURE OF SANCTIFICATION. The words used for holiness and sanctification carry with them the idea of separation. Sanctification, therefore, is first of all a separation from sin. It is not so much a cleansing of the natural heart as a separation from it, a putting it away altogether, a laying off of the old man and consigning him to death as unfit for existence and incapable of good. Most persons begin this search by trying to improve themselves. It is rather a getting rid of self, and then getting a new self in Christ. The picture Paul gives us in Colossians of this process of stripping is very fine. First, "Put off all these, anger, &c." Then, secondly ye have put off the old man, with his deeds." And then finally, "ye have put on the new man, which is renewed in knowledge after the image of Him that created him."

Sanctification is stripping off not merely the old clothes but the old flesh, the old self, stripping to the bone, stripping to the very core of the being, and daily reckoning self dead and keeping it out of all identification with it as we would with the corpse of a buried criminal.

Secondly, sanctification is separation TO GOD. It is not merely a negative thing, but a definite and voluntary self-dedication to God's ownership, possession, transformation and service. It involves the choice of a free and loving will, which chooses to be His, and puts itself into His hands, giving Him the right to rule it, and make of it the ideal of His own glorious will. This idea

138

of dedication runs through the whole Old Testament representations of sanctification. It underlies all the offerings and consecrations of the Mosaic ritual. It is involved in the New Testament idea of consecration. It is the giving of ourselves, a living sacrifice, holy, as acceptable unto God. This is the single eye, this is the idea of the "pure in heart, this is the meaning of a perfect heart, this is the meaning of the command, "Yield yourselves unto God." And when so presented, yielded, consecrated, God accepts the life, takes possession of it by His Holy Spirit, fills it with His own nature and holiness, and becomes its all-sufficient Keeper and Lord.

Then Christ, having taken possession of the heart, occupies it Himself, makes it His residence, and is made unto it of God sanctification, imparting to it day by day His own perfect life, transferring into it His own holiness, rest, confidence, strength and joy.

> "Jesus comes. He fills my soul;
> Perfected in Him I am."

III.

THE EXTENT OF OUR SANCTIFICATION: This passage represents it as entire. "That very God of peace sanctify you wholly," or "through and through." And then giving the particulars, in a sort of inventory of our whole threefold being, he adds: "Your whole spirit and soul and body." First, the spirit must be sanctified. This means the higher principle and element of our being, given us anew in regeneration, the upper chamber in the temple, looking out on God and eternity, the seat of conscience, will, trust, divine love, and all the graces of the new life. The conscience must be cleansed from guilt and error, and made to echo the voice of God and respond to the touch of the Holy Ghost. The will must be broken from its obstinacy, turned to God, and then divinely strengthened to choose and will after His good pleasure,

139

and with all the power of His own resistless will. The heart must be turned to God as the object of its supreme love and perfect trust, and find its delight and fellowship in His presence and communion, and the whole spirit be filled with the holy affections and heavenly graces of "love, joy, peace, long suffering, gentleness, goodness, faith, meekness, temperance."

Secondly, the soul, or seat of intellect, emotion, and sensibility itself, must be sanctified; the thoughts, ideas, opinions, judgments and ways of thinking, must all be brought into captivity to the obedience of Christ. The imagination must become subject to His holy touch and wait to carry on its wing His messages, and to paint with its magic hand only His pictures in the chambers of the soul. The memory must forget its old images, and hold His words and thoughts and wait as the handmaid of service with its stores of truth and promise. The emotions and sensibilities must turn from their capricious wandering and unregulated license and follow the bidding of conscience, will and the love of God. The affections must fall in line with God's love, and yield all their tender vines and tendrils to be trained on the walls of His temple in His sweet order and beauty, and live only in Him and for Him. The faculties must cease to work for their own gratification or pride, and become the handmaid of Christ in all His will and work. Such is a faint outline of a soul sanctified wholly in thought, imagination, feeling and affection, and every power and faculty of the mind.

Thirdly, the body must be sanctified. Disease, infirmity, impure humors and morbid functions must be removed. The ancient priesthood had to be free from physical blemishes, and it is one of the devil's most grotesque distortions that disease is one of the elements of holiness.

Therefore, Divine Healing is part of the Gospel of Christ and the work of redemption and the spirit. But a
140

sanctified body is not only a sound, it is also a consecrated body. Eyes yielded only to see for Him and purified from viewing vanity and looking on sin; ears sanctified from hearing an uncharitable word, all unholy conversation, all defiling things; lips that are touched with coals of fire and speak only the words of the Holy Spirit, sanctified, from every idle, bitter, or foolish word; hands to work for Him whether in the Church or the world, with a consecrated and quickened touch; feet that are ready to go on any of his errands, and that walk not in the paths or companionship of evil, and every member, organ and function so yielded to him that he fill it with His life, use it for His service, and make it a link of communion with the soul. O, the blessedness! O, the power! O, the quickened heavenly life of such a union with the body of Jesus Christ. Every physical function becomes a channel of spiritual blessing. Our eating, our drinking, our taste and smell, and sight and hearing all become avenues of entrance for all His heavenly retinue to enter the soul and spirit; and the whole being in new divine harmony, is conscious of being the dwelling place of God, and in partnership, a member not only of His deeper nature, but also of His body, His flesh, and His bones, we can say: "The life of Christ is made manifest in our mortal flesh." In such a life the body cannot be common or unclean. Its feeblest members have most abundant honor. It walks the earth with a delightful sacredness and purity, and as the temple of the Holy Ghost, seeks to glorify God and reflect His radiant Presence.

Now, this is God's picture of holiness, our entire threefold nature separated from sin, yielded to God and filled with His holy life and presence. Is it yours? Are you sanctified through and through? Are your bodies converted, saved, and filled as well as your spirits? Are your souls and intellects all the Lord's? Are your spirits filled with His Spirit? "The very God of Peace sanctify you *wholly*."

IV.

THE DIVINE METHOD OF SANCTIFICATION: – "The very God of Peace sanctify you;" or "The God of Peace HIMSELF sanctify you." It is God who sanctifies us. It is Himself who becomes in us the sanctity. It is the same sweet Gospel. "Christ made unto us sanctification." There is none good but one, that is God, and of His goodness must we all partake. "Partakers of the Divine nature" is the Divine theory of holiness. Man's holiness is poor stuff. We are called to Divine Holiness.

It is as the God of peace that He does it. There must be perfect reconciliation, and absolute confidence in His love. The soul must be yielded up to His Hand without a quiver of distrust, fear or resistance. Then shall the Engraver's Hand trace the faintest lines and perform His choicest handiwork without hindrance.

V.

OUR PRESERVATION IN HOLINESS "Preserved blameless." "There are two stages." "Sanctified" and "preserved." Now the second is as necessary as the first. We are not all at once and forever completed and stereotyped in our spiritual character, or set in motion like an automaton, but we are only attached to the source of life and power, and must keep open the communication moment by moment. It is life by the moment. In the vision of Zechariah the lamps of God are fed from the living olive trees, which as they ripen their fruit press out and pour in the oil into the bowls of the lamps. So on either side of us stand the Living Jesus and the Living Spirit, constantly providing and pouring in their life and sweetness into the soul and body of the abiding disciple. And thus we are preserved.

142

But we must abide in Him. It is not a state but a life. It is not an experience but a person. It is not a life in ourselves but a life in Him. "He that abideth in Him sinneth not." "Who are kept by the power of God through faith unto salvation."

> "He that hath made thee whole
> Will heal thee day by day.
> He that hath spoken to thy soul
> Hath many things to say.
> He that Himself hath taught,
> Yet none will make Thee known.
> He that so wondrously hath wrought
> Hath greater things to show,
> He loveth ever, faileth never,
> So trust in Him, the same forever."

VI.

THE GREAT INCENTIVE TO OUR ENTIRE SANCTIFICATION "unto the coming of our Lord." This, as we have seen, is the great theme of this Epistle. It is presented first as the incentive which led the heathen to turn from idols, to serve the living and true God, and to wait for His Son from Heaven. It is presented next as the faithful minister's great motive for service. "What is our joy or crown of rejoicing are not even ye in the presence of our Lord Jesus Christ at His coming. It is next unfolded as the ground of consolation for the bereaved, the blessed reunion of the parted ones in the air, when He shall come and we shall be "caught up together with them." And now here it is regarded as the great end which we are to prepare by a life of holiness.

Again and again is the subject of holy living presented in close connection with Christ's second coming. The parable of the ten virgins is a special warning of the doom of a slumbering and unsanctified church at His appearing. In the Apocalypse again and again we are

143

warned of the rejection and judgment that awaits the worldly, unholy and slothful, when He shall come, and the necessary preparation for the bride of Christ. "If thou shalt not watch I will come upon thee as a thief, and thou shalt not know what hour I will come upon thee." "Behold, I come quickly; hold that fast which thou hast that no man take thy crown!" " Behold, I come as a thief! blessed is he that watcheth and keepeth his garments lest he walk naked, and they see his shame." "The marriage of the Lamb is come, and His wife hath made herself ready, and to her it was granted that she should be arrayed in fine linen, clean and white; the white raiment is the righteousness of the saints." "Those are they that have not defiled themselves with women, and in their mouth was found no guile, for they are without spot before the throne of God."

Then there is the solemn parable of the talents, and also of the pounds, with their awful intimation about the unfaithful servants who were not ready to meet his Lord, and went forth to darkness from His bar. This is not the last judgment, but the judgment of the King at His first appearing. Is there not a lurid light cast on the prospects of the unholy and unfaithful? Perhaps it is not hell. But may it not be the great tribulation that is to immediately follow the master's appearing. Would it not be terrible to be left even to its brief horrors, although at last we did escape as by fire? And would it not be blessed, indeed, to be ready to meet Him with your welcome, and go in and sup with Him, above the storm, above the terrors of that dreadful day. Is He not now calling for His bride? Is He not now saying: "Behold! the bridegroom cometh, go ye out to meet Him?"

> "Are you ready for the Bridegroom,
>   When He comes, when He comes.
> Be robed and ready
>   For the Bridegroom comes."

144

He that *overcometh*, shall sit with Me on my throne."
"He that *overcometh*, shall inherit all things." "He that
overcometh I will confess his name before my Father and
His holy angels." God is linking together in these last
days very solemnly three things – viz., Divine holiness,
divine healing, and the Lord's coming. Surely the
connection is not accidental. They are interlinked in
mutual and solemn relationship, and are the overlapping
of the coming age. Let us know our times, and prepare
for the times that are so near at hand. Let us call men to
righteousness and faith in God. The two characteristics
of Daniel's picture of the end are: "Many shall be tried
and made white and purified." And "They that turn
many to righteousness shall shine as the stars for ever
and ever." Let the cry go forth. BE RIGHT WITH GOD,
THE LORD IS AT HAND.

VII.

THE GREAT ENCOURAGEMENT TO SANCTIFICATION.
"Faithful is he that calleth you, who also will do it." God
is not only willing to sanctify you wholly, He has
determined to. Only let Him. Let the clay lie on the
wheel, and the potter's hands will mould it. Let the soul ·
be yielded, and Christ will do His work. You can trust
His faithfulness, His love, His will. He is not capricious,
reluctant and remote. He longs to see you as pure as
Himself, and is just as ready to wash your stains away as
a mother loves to keep her babe spotlessly clean. But we
must meet His faithfulness with our unfaltering faith.
We must believe that He does sanctify and will help. We
must take His word. "Now are ye clean through the
word, that I have spoken to you" without rebate and
questioning. We must give ourselves unreservedly and
take Him as irrevocably. And as we do, the words will
fall from the throne,

"IT IS DONE,
BEHOLD, I MAKE ALL THINGS NEW!"

Is it not here that we have often lost our blessing. We have hungered, we have yielded, we have waited, and then we have questioned, and He has done according as we doubted. Has He not said, "Surely, if ye will not believe, ye shall not be established." And has He not said, "If thou canst believe all things are possible to Him that believeth." Let us trust Him. Let us take Him at His word for entire sanctification, and then "FAITHFUL IS HE THAT CALLETH YOU WHO ALSO WILL DO IT."

"He that calleth you." Yes, He hath called you, called you today. "The Master is come and calleth for thee." Hovering above you is a soft and gentle wing and a whispered message. "Behold the Bridegroom cometh, go ye out to meet Him." You are invited to the marriage of the Lamb, the greatest occasion the world shall ever see. Will you come, will you prepare? Will you put on your wedding garments? Will you be there, "robed in whiteness, clad in brightness?" Or will you be without?

Well, at least you have been called. The answer you must give. Amen.

THESSALONICA.

CHAPTER XIII

CHRISTIAN LIFE IN TIMOTHY AS EXEMPLIFIED IN ST. PAUL.

"I have fought a good fight, I have finished my course, I have kept the faith: Henceforth there is laid up for me a crown of righteousness, which the Lord, the righteous judge, shall give me at that day: and not to me only, but unto all them also that love his appearing." – 2 Tim. 4: 7-8.

*L*ET US LOOK this morning at the character of Paul as portrayed in the epistles to Timothy. "Be ye followers of me as I also am of Christ" was the bold yet humble language of this great Apostle to the Gentiles, to the Corinthian church. There is exquisite beauty in the thought that Paul was here holding up only the personal character of Jesus. It was as if the Lord Jesus had taken His own precious character and transfused it into the character of Paul, and made a copy of Himself, a miniature as it were, which would be made within our reach, more on our own level, more really and entirely human. Both characters are divine, Paul's as well as Christ's, but Paul's is divine life in a man who had once been a sinful lost man, and, therefore, it is at a standpoint that any one can come to.

We shall not attempt to go over this morning all the points in Paul's life, but touch only on a few that come out in these epistles.

I.

His was a life redeemed from great sin. At the very beginning of the first epistle, 1 Tim. 1:15, he says: "This is a faithful saying and worthy of all acceptation, that Christ Jesus came into the world to save sinners: of whom I am chief." A little further back in the chapter he gives this truth with more detail, and says he obtained mercy because he did it ignorantly in himself. It would seem as though God had selected Paul as a sample of what He can do for men, because he was not only a sinner, but the worst of sinners. There is no doubt but this language is true, for the Holy Ghost was speaking through Paul, and he would not have let him say that if it were not true. I believe Paul provoked God more than any other man. He should have known better. Oh, how marvelous that out of the vilest and most lost wrecks that lie broken upon the shore of life God prepares His vessels for honor and glory! How wonderful that He can take souls that have been steeped in sin and make them shine as the stars forever and ever. He took this depth of iniquity and evil, this capability of wrong in Paul, and turned it into means of service to others. Such souls are used as shining lights. There are threads of sympathy in them that make them feel for all men, even the most lost and sinful. Saying to the fallen: "I was once lost, and I know you are not too lost to be saved." Henceforth the chief of sinners was as zealous in his work for God as he had previously been against him. He was now a most earnest follower – because his former life had been so much at variance with Christ. How he desired to be more avenged on the enemy because he had been so greatly under his power. There is an element of great encouragement in this for those of God's children who have been greatly under the control of Satan. Some of His most useful servants have been made from such men. They have been saved from great sin and brought into a deep, personal experience with their Redeemer, and then made chosen vessels to others that they may not only glorify their dear Master, but encourage all classes of sinners to come to Him.

150

Paul was an example of great grace. 1Tim. 1:14. "The grace of God was exceeding abundant with faith and love, which is in Christ Jesus." He was not only redeemed, but he entered at once into a rich and deep experience of the grace of Christ, a grace which forgave, healed, purified, sanctified and lifted him up and strengthened him. Yet this experience was just as human as yours and mine. We are apt to think the inspired men of the Bible had help which we have not got. Paul had no unusual grace because he was inspired. Paul had to take the same strength for his every day life that you and I need. He was inspired to write the epistle, but he needed grace just as much to make him able to walk day by day without blame before God. He had to learn the secret of success in these things and get a revelation of himself and of his Master in him as much as you and I do. If you will study his letters carefully you will see that every step of his onward life was as much weary up hill work as yours or mine, and he had many a conflict and many a stumble before he could say: "I have kept the faith." After the Lord met him so wondrously at Damascus he was sent down into the desert of Arabia for three years, and alone in that solitary place was undoubtedly taught many precious lessons from his dear Master. He gives us a part of his experience in the epistle to the Romans. Many of you know what it means, for you have been through it. "I was alive once without the law; but when the commandment came, sin revived and I died." The conflict was too strong for him and he gave up for a while, thinking it was no use to try any longer. He began to see that there was in him a desire to be good, there was no power to overcome the evil, and in despair he cried out, "Oh! wretched man that I am." He felt as if he had fastened to him a dead corpse, a horrid body of putrefaction which he could not shake off. Then he suddenly got a view of Jesus standing by him and knew there was deliverance for him in Him. Beloved, have you had this view of your Saviour, and have you heard Him say "I am as able to do this for thee as for Paul?" Christ has suffered for all, and He is as able to give this blessed rest to us as He was to him. John tells us how sweet it is to lean on Jesus' breast, but he cannot tell us as Paul can how to get there. The epistles to the Ephesians, Philippians and Colossians teach us how to live in Christ. Paul tells us as no other Apostle does of Christ within us the hope of glory, Christ who is all and in all, Christ who shall supply every need, and it is Paul who is able to give us in his last moments that glad song of triumph. "I have kept, not the commandment, or the experience, but the *faith*, which is the sum and substance of all experience.

III.

Paul's was a life greatly endued by the Holy Ghost with power for service. 2Tim. 1:17. "For God had not given us the spirit of fear; but of power and of love, and of a sound mind." This enduement was to enable him to carry forward Christian life and work. It was not an experience but a divine baptism that came on him, sufficient for his life work. So when fully given up to God, does the Holy Spirit always come upon the humble follower of Christ with sufficient power for all his service.

1. It brought to him the spirit of courage. He had to learn confidence and trust. He did not allow himself to be pressed by a single question or doubt. He never knew a fear. It is said of Nelson when but a child his mother asked him once if he was not afraid in a dangerous place he had been in. "Mama," he said, "I don't know what you mean by fear," and he fell at last without a fear, in
152

that great victory which won for England the supremacy of the seas. So also this intrepid soldier of the cross did not know fear. With his eye upon his Master, thinking only of pleasing Him, he might be in the midst of false brethren, or foes that pressed on every side, but he trusted unflinchingly through it all and came off more than conqueror. Paul came through unparalleled suffering of every kind, yet he held the faith firm unto the end. He could not listen to fears while clothed with the power of God. We cannot get through life without invincible courage. Nehemiah said his enemies tried to make him fear that he might sin. Whenever we are afraid we sin. Beloved, we must have the inspiration of courage if we are to walk in the footsteps of Paul, and we can only have it by breathing in more of the Holy Ghost.

2. Paul had the enduement of power. Perhaps more than any Christian who ever lived he had the power of God resting on his work. It was a real power that took root and produced transformation of character in himself and filled his work with success. Beloved, we must have this divine power if our work is to be fruitful and effectual, and our lives are to tell for God.

3. He had the spirit of love. His life was exquisitely interwoven with tenderness and affection. Look at his language to his beloved fellow workers, dearer to him than if united by the ties of human affection, or bone of his bone and flesh of his flesh. He had an intensely affectionate nature, but it was divine love that filled him not the natural love for relatives. He was cut off from all these, but it was the love of God which filled his heart for all those who loved their common Lord. How sweetly he speaks of his son Timothy, the beloved Persis, Phebe our sister, and many others. How his heart went out too for those who tried to hinder him. Through all their opposition he pressed on and tried to save them. How tender his language to Mark who had at one time been a little lacking in courage, but who was instantly taken

153

back to Paul's heart as soon as he took up his work again. All the old wound is healed, and he writes: "Bring Mark, for he is profitable to me for the ministry." And oh! how wonderful his love for souls. Hear him say: "I could wish myself accursed from Christ for my brethren." His very soul was poured out like water for them, so that he could even wish to perish that they might be saved. What an example of love is dear old Paul. Beloved, we are nothing without it. Oh, for more of this precious gift of the Holy Ghost.

4. Paul was also endowed with wisdom. How wise he was, yet how foolish the people thought him. How he hated the wisdom of this world and set his face against it, but the wisdom which is from above was given him for his work. The divine wisdom in the Holy Ghost to win souls was his in a remarkable degree. Under its guidance he mapped out the whole world as if he had been bishop of it all, and there grew up in his mind those five great missionary journeys in which he swept through the entire known world to win it for Christ. His friends did not always understand his course. When he was at Cæsarea, Philip the evangelist tried to keep him back from the course God had told him to go in, and even Agabus, a prophet of the Lord, felt he was inspired to prophecy against his going. But Paul went straight on to Jerusalem, saying to the dear friends who tried to hinder him "God has spoken to me and showed me my path. You cannot now be my conscience." And so they ceased, saying "The *will of the Lord* be done." They let Paul go on and obey God's word when they thought they had God's wisdom themselves. He went on, through suffering indeed, but he reached the world. He never would have reached Rome if he had allowed other voices to disturb him. But God had spoken and he did not dare to disobey. What a pattern he becomes to us. This wisdom he had can be ours, and if we obey it as he did,

we shall be able to say at the last like Paul, "I have finished my course, not one thing has been left undone."

IV.

Paul's was a life of great service. The story of his labors is the story of aggressive Christianity in the early church. His first great work was not planned according to human wisdom, but was of divine origin. It was the great church at Antioch, very much like our own here in its object. It was a great center from which the work branched out in many directions. It was like a mother caring for many children, a starting point from which other churches of the same kind could be planted, and so the work was able to extend to other cities and lands. It was not like the church at Jerusalem, but it was the first free church, including in its membership Jews and Gentiles, black and white, every nationality and class that would come under its protection.

From this earnest body of Christians, Paul, taking with him his noble brother Barnabas, filled with the Holy Ghost, went forth on his first missionary journey. They passed through the island of Cyprus and then proceeded to Asia Minor, where they preached Jesus in many of the cities, and then returned to the mother church at Antioch to tell of the wondrous working of God upon the hearts of the people they had met.

In the second journey which he undertook not long after, he skirted the same parts of Asia Minor and then passed on to the shores of Europe, stopping at Philippi, Thessalonica and Corinth, and establishing there the great European church from which the gospel was afterwards carried far westward.

In the third journey he landed at Ephesus, then the commercial capital of the East, and preached there for three years. From this point which was the depot of transportation from Africa, the religion of Jesus passed over into Africa and the churches of Alexandria and Carthage were established from which Christianity spread into the center of Africa. These great African churches have given to the world such prominent Christian names as Augustine and Athanasius.

After this Paul went to Jerusalem. His friends tried to hold him back, but they could not, for the voice of God had bidden him to go on to the very capital of the world, and on he went through storms and imprisonments, across the perilous sea, on through the hate of men and the opposition of Satan, till at last he reached the goal his eyes had so long been fixed on – Rome. Before three centuries had rolled away this capital of the world had also become the capital of the Christian church, and all because of Paul. It is wonderful to think what one man accomplished with no missionary society back of him, no port, no letters, no money, supporting himself part of the time by his own trade, and preaching only on the Sabbath day, and, perhaps in the evenings. Paul had no church at home to pay his way, he went with no recommendation except that of a nuisance and a fool, yet what a glorious work he did in Asia Minor, in Greece, in Ephesus and finally at Rome, and toward the end of his life probably in Spain and Illyricum. All the world nearly he had traversed, mostly on foot in that hot climate, often weary, yet always rejoicing. His labors were prodigious. He could truly say "I labored more abundantly than they all." Every point of the great work he had mapped out was reached. It is glorious to come to the end of one's work in that way. The Lord knew the dream of his youth. He had fulfilled the longing of his manhood. He had indeed enabled him to finish his course with joy. Beloved, are we coming to the end of our work in this way? If we have set our faces to it like a flint, we shall. The same power that so marvelously prospered Paul, the same protecting care that preserved him in the midst of danger and trial are as freely offered to you and to me.

V.

Paul's was a life of great suffering. 2Tim. 1:8-15. The hardest blow Paul ever got was when he knew all in Asia were turned away from him where he had lived and labored for three years, where the elders of the church at Ephesus sorrowed over him as over a father and friend, falling on his neck and kissing him as he left them to go to Jerusalem. All had turned away from him. It was the same with dear old John on Patmos. He wrote unto the church, but Diotrephes received him not. It was not popular to follow him. The church had become proud and self-willed. They were prejudiced against the dear old saint, and ashamed to follow him in his bonds.

Again, 2Tim. 3:11, he speaks of persecutions that befell him in other places out of which the Lord delivered him. There is not a bit of morbidness in the way he speaks of them. He sorrows only that they are losing who thus persecuted him. Shortly after he writes: Demas hath forsaken me. Then he sends for his old cloak he left at Troas. Why did he want that? Because it was winter at Rome, and he was lying half naked in a damp, cold dungeon, and he needed his old cloak. He was now Paul the prisoner of the Lord, the fellow-sufferer of Jesus Christ. He went through suffering of every kind. He had been in perils from robbers, in perils from wild beasts, in perils on the briny deep, beaten with rods till his body was crushed almost to a jelly, stoned nearly to death again and again, but in the face of it all he pressed on. Sickness swept over him so that he despaired even of life, the devil tried to take away his strength, but God delivered him; yes, and he will yet deliver, was the cry of the old hero. Oh, beloved, when we think of our sufferings, we ought to be ashamed. What are they compared to Paul's?

VI.

Paul was a man of great faith and confidence in God. 2Tim. 1:12: "I know whom I have believed." He not only knew about Him, but He knew Him well. Christ was not only with him, but He was in Him, and Paul knew He would keep what he had committed to Him, and would give all back to him when he looked in His face at that day. Not anything would be left out. He would find it all in that last day. How marvelously his faith speaks out in the eighteenth verse of the fourth chapter: "The Lord shall deliver me from every evil work." How firmly he was able to stand and do his work with this assurance in his heart. At Corinth, years before, he had received that precious promise, "no man shall set on thee to hurt thee," and Paul had not been afraid. So, too, had it been at Rome – he was delivered out of the mouth of the lion. That may have been Nero, or it may have been a real lion in the Coliseum. I do not know which was the worse lion, but its mouth was shut. This sublime faith is for you and me as well as for Paul, if we are in the path the Lord has called us in. He shall deliver us from every evil work. Say it, looking right into His face, no matter what the evil work. The difficulty shall disappear as the sand is washed away by the incoming tide. Have you said it? Has your heart said it? If so, the heavens have answered back: "The Lord shall deliver you from every evil work." That is faith, that is being more than conqueror through Him that loved us. No matter in what appalling way the devil may encamp against you, say: "I have nothing to do with the devil, the Lord shall deliver me." Oh, beloved, take hold of him with strong, earnest faith this morning, and you shall find, no matter how great your trial and need, the Lord is bigger than them all.

VII.

Paul had great prospects before him. *"Henceforth,"* he said. He had nothing to do with the past. Henceforth there is laid up for me a crown. He did not have to make a will. He had nothing to will away. His possessions were in heaven, where was laid up for him a crown of righteousness. There is a real recompense for us there. We do not deserve it, but he gives it as though we did. As the recompense of faithful service there shall be given to us a crown of righteousness at the second coming of our dear Lord. At the same moment we shall stand side by side with dear old Paul, and receive our crowns together. I am afraid ours will wither away very much. I am sure we shall think no teardrop has been too hot, no trial too long, no service too hard in that day.

Beloved, how is it with us now? How will it be then? Paul is saying to us again this morning: "Be ye followers of me, even as I also am of Christ." We have the same sins to be pardoned as he. There is the same abundant grace for us that he found. We, too, may have the same enduement of power and the same glorious service; not, perhaps, to evangelize the world, but in our place and calling. There is for us the same cup of suffering and trial, to be borne meekly and without complaint, so no one can know by our face or life that we are suffering. And there is laid up for us the same glorious crown at last. May the Lord make us faithful and inspire us this morning with new zeal for His work. The years are passing on and soon all will be over. Joyous youth, strong manhood, bright, fresh womanhood, golden opportunities, all will soon be gone. You will remember then how God came many times and made your heart beat with strange longing as he knocked there for admission, and now you are going yourself. "Oh," you will cry, "I thought I had plenty of time. Must I go, and empty handed?" Oh, think of it. I know it is hard to

159

stand firm at all times and be true to the trust He has given; hard to press on through good report and evil report, but I am so glad He enables us to do it. It is difficult to let this pleasure go and take less than we might have in life, difficult to press on to harder service when we might have taken the easier way – but, blessed be God, there is glorious victory in it all. It will be sweet to look back upon life and say: "If I had it all to live over again, I don't know how I could have lived it differently. Henceforth there is laid up for me a crown of righteousness." Some day the Master will come, and as we stand before Him there will be a calm, deliberate weighing of all that has been done. He will listen to all we have to say, and then what is left of true service for Him will receive its reward. Let us then work on, fight on, and trust, on knowing that He is able to keep that which we have committed to Him against that day.

CHAPTER XIV

FROM GRACE TO GLORY

"For the grace of God that bringeth salvation hath appeared to all men, Teaching us that, denying ungodliness and worldly lusts, we should live soberly, righteously, and godly, in this present world; Looking for that blessed Hope, and the glorious appearing of the great God and our Saviour Jesus Christ; Who gave Himself for us, that He might redeem us from all iniquity, and purify unto Himself a peculiar people, zealous of good works." – Titus 2:11-14.

THREE stages and aspects of Grace are here unfolded.

I. – GRACE IN OUR SALVATION.

"The grace of God that bringeth salvation to all men hath appeared." This does not mean, of course, that all men will be absolutely saved by Divine grace, irrespective of their personal faith and character, but that: –

1. Grace has provided an atonement adequate for the sins of all men. "For God so loved the world that He gave His only Begotten Son that whosoever believeth in Him might not perish but have eternal life."

2. Grace offers salvation to every man, without distinction of class or character, on the simple condition of receiving and believing. "Go ye into all the world and preach the gospel to every creature."

3. Grace takes the most worthless and gives them salvation without money and without price. It does not wait until they earn it, but meets them a great way off

161

and takes them from the very start on simple trust, not because of anything in them but only because of its own nature. "Would you be my loyal subject if I should exercise grace instead of justice and forgive your crime?" said Queen Elizabeth to her would-be assassin. "That, Madam, would be no grace at all, to found your grace on the condition of my merit." "Then I pardon you unconditionally," said the Queen. "That," replied the proud French woman, as she clasped her feet, "that is queenly Grace, and now I am your slave for life." So grace takes us and conquers.

4. Grace takes the most helpless and supplies all their need and helplessness with divine strength and goodness. It does not "help the man that helps himself," but it helps the man who cannot help himself. It touches his hard, cold heart with the drawings of the Spirit. It meets him out on the mountains and carries him home, rejoicing. It shines in upon his dark heart and reveals to him the person and grace of Jesus. And, if his will accepts the gracious offer, it comes to give him the spirit of penitence and trust, to enable him to believe and receive the Saviour, to freely justify and forgive his transgressions, to cover him with the righteousness of Christ and make him "accepted in the Beloved," to breathe into his soul the life of regeneration and the first impulses of the new nature, and to offer to the returning prodigal the best robe, the ring, the shoes, the feast and the fellowship of the Father's house, so that the sinner need not stay away till he has a deep repentance, a perfect faith, and a new heart to bring the Lord. Christ has all these to give. All he needs to bring is a sense of need, and a willingness to receive. And he never will have anything good until he comes.

5. And grace not only receives the poor helpless sinner, but it keeps him, leads him and enables him to stand. "By whom also we have access by faith into this grace wherein we stand." The widow's oil is not only

162

sufficient to pay her debt, but also to "live upon the rest."
The Father's house is not only a refuge, but also a home,
and the house is as free as the first welcome.

Such is salvation by grace alone – the gift of God
through our Lord Jesus Christ." All our struggling,
suffering, serving cannot win it, but the grace of God is
glad to give it to all who will receive it. A poor Scottish
mother had come from the bedside of her sick and
suffering child. She passed the gardens of the Queen,
and as she saw the luscious clusters hanging from the
vines, she stepped up to the gardener and, holding out a
handful of silver, asked if she might buy some for her
child. The gardener looked up with a stern face and said,
"This is the Queen's Garden, and the Queen never sells
her grapes." But just that moment the gentle Queen
walked through the greenhouse and saw and overheard
the little scene, and with a mother's heart she turned to
the woman and said, "The Queen never sells her grapes,
but she will be glad to give you as many as you need,"
and, turning to the gardener, she ordered him to fill her
apron and take them to her dying child, with the love of
her Queen. So grace gives but will not sell its costliest
treasures.

II. – THE GRACE THAT SANCTIFIES.

"Teaching us that denying ungodliness and worldly
lusts, we should live soberly, righteously and godly in
this present world." "He gave Himself for us that He
might redeem us from all iniquity and purify unto
Himself a peculiar people zealous of good works."

1. The design of His redemption was our sanctification.
He gave Himself for us that He might redeem us, not
only from the curse, but from all iniquity. He did not
give Himself for us merely to check the power of sin, but
wholly to destroy it. But this is only the negative side.
Holiness is not being cleansed from sin and left an empty

163

void, but it is a positive dedication of our life to Christ as His own personal possession and devoted to His service. This is the meaning of the expression to purify us unto Himself, that is to separate us in singleness of purpose unto Himself, a peculiar people, or rather a people for personal possession. His own and only His, and as such zealously devoted to His will and work. This is the very end of Christ's death, and if it has not been realized in you. He has so far been disappointed.

2. Our practical part in the accomplishment of this great purpose of redemption is likewise both negative and positive. "Denying ungodliness and worldly lusts," that is saying no to everything in us which would ignore, forsake or disobey God, and saying no likewise to every impulse and desire which would draw us to the world or terminate upon ourselves or our own gratification; we should next positively "live soberly, righteously and godly in this present world." These three words describe very distinctly our obligations to ourselves, our neighbor, and our God. The first is a proper self-restraint, the second a right relationship and action to all others, and the third is a right attitude to God, and covers all the religious affections and exercises of the highest spiritual life.

This is Christian holiness, practical, comprehensive, all-inclusive, and intensely real.

3. Next, we have the actual process of inworking this holiness into our life. "Teaching us." That is, grace teaches us. The word means literally *disciplining* us, putting us to school, and patiently and tenderly instilling into us these lessons over and over, day by day, until we know and live them.

Now, let it be carefully remembered that it is grace and not works that is doing all this, that it is all freely given and not painfully wrought out of our self life, that it is Christ's grace bestowed upon us to meet the spiritual consequences of every day and hour, rather than our

164

wisdom, strength and vigilance, and yet to know how to receive it, use it, apply it to the temptations and needs of every day, requires God's most patient discipline and gentle teaching.

For example, you all know the difference between the process of making a painting by hand and transferring it through the simple art of *Decalcomania*. The one is your own work; the other is simply transferred. So in our Christian life the pictures are all transferred. They are supplied to us, and we have but to put them into their places in the work of life. And yet the transferring of a French picture is no easy, trifling task, but needs much caution and care. And in our daily life the Holy Spirit is continually teaching us the Divine act of putting on the grace of Christ Jesus. For example, one day the need is love. And so the blessed Spirit leads you into situations where you must have a great deal of love, and you find you have not got it. Human nature fails, and shows, perhaps, anything but a spirit of love. This is the very time for grace to come in. And so the Spirit reveals to you the love and grace of Christ, offered to you for this very need and time. And you accept it, open your heart to it, claim it, and go forth under the blessed baptism of Divine love to overcome. The next day it may be patience. If so, you will be sure to find an unusual number of trials, and you shall probably find the same old story of failure. But you will be reminded that you may have "the meekness and gentleness of Christ" instead of your impatience, and so again, putting on the Lord Jesus, and claiming His indwelling spirit as your power to overcome, and glorify Him in every trial, you again go forward and find His grace sufficient. Next it will be the grace of courage that is to be transferred and exercised. So you find yourself confronted by unusual difficulties. Your spirit shrinks and falters; your courage fails. But it is the very time for His. You must now learn that you have One to fall back upon who said, "I have set my face like a flint, and I know that I shall not be ashamed." And, conscious of new weakness, you claim His courage, and as the Spirit touches your heart from on high, the cowardly sinner of the judgment hall is changed into Peter of Pentecost and you too can say, "Behold the Lord God is with me, who shall contend with me. I have set my face like a flint, and I know that I shall not be ashamed."

Thus we learn to receive "grace for grace," and "giving all diligence to add to our faith courage, knowledge, temperance, patience, godliness, brotherly kindness, charity; and when these are in us and abound, they make us that we be neither barren nor unfruitful in the knowledge of our Lord Jesus Christ; but so an entrance shall be ministered unto us abundantly into the everlasting Kingdom of our Lord and Saviour Jesus Christ."

III. – GRACE AND GLORY.

"Looking for that blessed Hope, and the glorious appearing of the great God and, our Saviour Jesus Christ."

Not only does grace provide for all the needs of our earthly life, but it is laying up for us an inheritance incorruptible, undefiled, and that fadeth not away. There is an expression in the Second Chapter of Ephesians in connection with Paul's picture of grace which shines like a pole star in the firmament of the future: "That in the ages to come He might show the exceeding riches of His grace in His kindness to us by Christ Jesus. For by grace ye are saved through faith, and that not of yourselves; it is the gift of God."

This passage reminds us that

> "There are heights of grace that we cannot know
>   Till we cross the narrow sea."

166

That all that grace is doing for us now is but as a drop to the ocean in comparison with the things it is preparing for us at the coming of Jesus Christ.

There is another passage in the first Epistle of Peter which bids us "be sober and hope to the end for the grace that is to be brought unto us at the revelation of Jesus Christ."

What is this grace?

1. It is a great and gracious thing that we should be taught this blessed hope which so many have never known or realized, the coming of our Lord.

2. Its influence on our present life is most blessed and gracious, separating from the world, arming against temptation and uplifting the heart in trial and sorrow.

3. But all this is as nothing to the blessing it is to bring in the hour of its glorious fulfillment, for then it will bring such glorious light on all the darkness of the past. It will show us how many of the things that tried and perplexed us were big with mercy and disguises for divine grace. It will bring into our full view the times innumerable when grace alone saved us from falling, and held us back from disasters and perils we never knew. It will bring the healing of all the sorrows of the past, and wipe every tear away forever. It will bring us the fulness and perfection of our spiritual life, and we shall know that we bear indeed and forever the perfect likeness of our Lord. Then the weakest and most discouraged disciple shall shine forth like the sun in the kingdom of our Father. Then the soul that oft has been so blamed, and blamed itself still more shall be presented by Christ Himself, faultless before the presence of His Father's glory with exceeding joy. Then shall our knowledge grasp the secrets of infinity, our hearts rest on the bosom of eternal peace, our deepest longings be satisfied, and our mighty activities have absolute and boundless scope and delightful employ. Then shall our bodies spring up into immortal youth and tireless energy, and wear the

beauty and glory of His majesty. Then shall the tides of buoyant health leap forth in eternal youth and freshness and life be indeed a joy forever. Then shall weeping love dry its briny tears and clasp its dearest treasures without a thought of parting or a fear of death. Then shall we know each other with a fellowship like that with which we know Him now, and Love weave its golden girdle about us all forever. Then shall we meet the best and noblest spirits of time and eternity, and sit with Gabriel, Elijah and John at Jesus' side. But best of all we shall see Jesus, we shall be with Him and like Him, and we shall be satisfied.

The external surroundings shall be the least of our joys, but they shall be worthy of the omnipotence of God and the redeeming blood. Then we shall know something of the value of the blood, which bought us and did all this for us. Then we shall wonder often at the tears and fears of time, and the little we dared to ask of Him who shall have given us all this princely glory. Then we shall see and adore the victory of grace over the wrath of Satan and the ravages of sin, and often realize the truth of the words, "that where sin abounded grace doth much more abound." Once in a dark and trying hour, while waiting at a railway depot far from home, like a whisper from Heaven, like a far off vision that touched the heart to something deeper than tears, came these heavenly words, "THAT IN THE AGES TO COME HE MIGHT SHOW THE EXCEEDING RICHES OF HIS GRACE IN HIS KINDNESS TO US THROUGH CHRIST JESUS." It seemed to lift the eye onward a millennium of years, and in the strange impalpable unuttered glory of the vision sorrow and pain seemed to melt away. So let it fall on your heart today. Lift up your eyes to "the ages to come" and forget the trials of today, and be encouraged to claim sufficient grace for today as you contemplate "the exceeding riches" of "the grace that is to be brought unto you at the revelation of Jesus Christ." "For the Lord God is a sun

168

and shield. He will give grace and glory. No good thing will He withhold from them that walk uprightly."

"When we reach our Father's dwelling,
    On the strong eternal hills,
And our praise to Him is swelling,
    Who the vast creation fills.
Shall we then recall the sadness,
    And the clouds that hang so dim;
When our hearts are turned from hardness,
    And our feet from paths of sin.

"Shall we then recall the story
    Of our mortal griefs and fears,
When on earth we sought the glory
    Wrestling oft with doubts and fears.
Yes, we surely shall remember,
    And His grace will freely own ;
For the love so strong and tender,
    That redeemed and brought us home.

"All the way by which He brought us ;
    All the grievings that He bore ;
All the patient love that taught us,
    We'll "remember ever more."
And His rest will be the dearer,
    As we think of weary ways.
And His light will be the clearer,
    As we muse on cloudy days."

CHAPTER XV.

CHRISTIAN LIFE IN HEBREWS

"Let us labor therefore to enter into that rest." – Heb. 4:11.

"For by one offering He hath perfected forever them that are sanctified." – Heb. 10:14.

"Looking unto Jesus the author and finisher of our faith." – Heb. 12:2.

---

*T*HESE THREE VERSES give the three great topics of the Epistle to the Hebrews, which unfolds the life of the believer in deeper fellowship with Jesus through the Holy Ghost. Rest is the first great theme of Christian life in the epistle. It expresses a whole universe of blessing, and meets a whole infinitude of need in us. The second is perfection. This meets the great demand of God's perfect nature and the great need of man. The last and most comprehensive is faith looking unto Jesus. Faith has reached its climax and its crown there. These are three great steps in a great ladder, and although so great and mighty, they are low enough for you and me to ascend.

All the epistles and books of the New Testament present different phases of Christian life. Not one of them is repeated in the others. This epistle is not Galatians, or Philippians, or Colossians. The truths they express are just as important, but they are different. They are like a beautiful cluster of hills that together form a mountain range. They are each covered with green, and glorious, yet none of them are alike. Look at them in Scotland, or Switzerland, or in the grand Sierras. God never made two of them alike. Each is beautiful, yet they are endlessly distinct. Not even the clouds floating in the sky are alike in form. So with God's pictures of character. Man's are all alike. He holds up one pattern, and says: "Look at this and be like it." Not so with God. He has a thousand types that are completed and filled up in our life pattern. This morning we have three sides of Christian character before us.

I. – REST.

The writer of this epistle takes two chapters to define and apply this subject: the third and fourth. He goes back to the story of creation and then on to the time when the children of Israel entered Canaan.

1. The first is God's rest after the work of creation was finished – a type of our rest after our work is over. God is full of rest as of labor. He is mighty, yet He is always in repose. He is full of majestic power, yet always still and undisturbed. Like the ocean that tosses its great arms up to the sky while its heart underneath is as still as a stone, so God's heart is ever at rest, even in the midst of His busy work. Oh, that we might be more and more filled with His rest. How it would still all our unrest and fretting; how it would calm all the paroxysms of our natural life, the wild impulses of the human heart, and fill us with the blessedness of rest.

God's rest did not come till after His work was over, and ours will not. We begin our Christian life by working, trying to keep the law, struggling in the energy of the flesh to save ourselves. For a long time it is nothing but work, work, work. At last, when we are able to cease from our own work. God comes in with His blessed rest, and works His own divine works in us.

2. The conquest of Canaan by Joshua is also a type of rest. But some of the children of Israel did not enter in because of unbelief. "But with whom was He grieved forty years? Was it not with them that had sinned, whose carcasses fell in the wilderness? And to whom sware He

172

that they should not enter into His rest, but to them that believed not?"

The land of Canaan as well as the Sabbath is a type of rest. We are accustomed to look at it as a type of heaven. Jordan has often been spoken of as a type of death, and the fields of Canaan, of the heavenly land. God never speaks of it so in His Word, but always as an example of the fulness of salvation. The real meaning of Canaan is the Christian rest, that comes to the soul that has left Egypt or the world, that has gone through the wilderness of unsatisfactory experience and occasional backward looks at Egypt, and has come to the Jordan and there died forever to self and renounced the natural will forever. Then Canaan can be entered, which is perfect rest in Jesus Christ through the Holy Ghost. Beloved, the land of Canaan is open to you all. If you are willing to wholly put down the self-life, you can enter the land filled with the resurrection life of Christ. Some of you, perhaps, may remember the time, years ago, when for days and weeks you were on the ocean. The time when it took three months to cross it can scarcely be remembered now. What a weary time it was. How one tired of the everlasting blue and green, and longed for the shore, for a sight of home, or even the land of strangers; and what joy filled the heart again as the eye rested on the habitations of men. So after forty years of wandering in the wilderness through the trackless sand and under the burning heat of the sun, with the skeletons of their fathers and mothers whitening on the ground around them, and passing on only to meet new graves in their march, the children of Israel at last beheld the fields of Canaan before them. What a blessed change it was. How sweet the rest that came to them. So, much more, after weary struggling and striving with self, after trying vainly to put down this loud, demoniac, wild nature which thinks every thing else is so wrong because our own heart is aching and restless, Jesus Christ shows Himself as rest

173

and peace. And as we open our heart and take Him in for these things, we have nothing to do but keep Him in. He does the conquering for us, and we have only to rest and rejoice in His work. Some of you have known this blessed presence for a while, and the memory lives with you as a joy greater than anything earth can give. You may have lost some of its sweetness, but you remember well when it first came thrilling into your heart and taking away your sense of guilt and consciousness of deserved wrath. Until there is this total surrender to God, the life is filled with foreboding and anxiety. The one great condition is to cast all your care on Him, and then not struggle to do, but know that He has done all and will do exceeding abundantly above all that you are able to ask or think, and now there is no need of trying and striving. Jesus has been taken into the life, and He will keep it pure and true. We are not only delivered from unrest, but we have God's rest in the heart. This is not mere passive inactivity. Many a person drops in apathetic inertia who is not at all at rest, but lies tossing in the waves of temptation and suffering. We may be intensely active, and yet have a heart as still as a babe's. This rest comes not because of stillness, but because the heart is full of harmony with those around, and is bounding with life and health. So the soul's rest is not a dead-and-alive passiveness, but it comes because the whole being is in harmony with God, and the heart is right with all around. You may dam up a river, but it will soon dash over the rocks and let you know how unhappy and restless it is. The rest of the river is in going on. The rest God gives is perfect accordance with His will, a yielding to every claim He makes, and a perfect satisfaction for every need of the heart. It is God's coming in and giving life and strength and peace.

The way to make the heart restful is not to stop its beating. Belladonna will do that, but that is not rest. Let the breath of life come – God's life and strength – and
174

there will be sweet rest. Home ties and family affection will not bring it. Deliverance from trouble will not give it. Many a tried heart has said: "If this great trouble was only gone, I should have rest." But as soon as one goes another comes. The poor, wounded deer on the mountain side thinks if it could only bathe in the old mountain stream it would have rest. But the arrow is in its flesh and there is no rest for it till the wound is healed. It is as sore in the mountain lake as on the plain. We shall never have God's rest and peace in the heart till we have given everything up to Christ, even our work, and believe He has taken it all and we have only to keep still and trust. It is necessary to walk in holy obedience and let Him have the government on His shoulder. Paul said: "This *one thing* I do." There is one narrow path for us all – Christ's will and work for us.

Dear friends, this is what you need more than anything else, and it is for you. This blessed Sabbath day is its glorious type. Jesus is saying to you all this morning: "Come unto Me, all ye that labor and are heavy laden, and I will rest you." "Take My yoke upon you, and learn of Me: for I am meek and lowly in heart: and ye shall find rest unto your souls. For My yoke is easy and burden is light." Oh, is there anything simpler or easier than that? That is the true Christian life, and it is an easy life. If you have not found it so, you have not taken His yoke upon you. You have not bowed to the meek and lowly One if you are filled with unrest. God help you, dear brethren, to do it. How sorry He is for that wounded heart and those limbs torn by the thorns. Ah, they were not found in the path He had marked out for you. You have got off the path, like the silly lamb, and found the briers and the fangs of the cruel wolf. May God give you His rest and make you willing to take it. "Let us therefore fear lest, a promise being left us of entering into His rest, any of you should seem to come short of it."

II. – PERFECTION

We now pass on to the second topic of the epistle. It runs through the whole epistle. We learn from Heb. 2: 10, that Jesus Himself was made perfect through suffering. He did not need it to make Him pure. He was pure before, but His life was matured, filled up by suffering. In the same sense our lives are made perfect by suffering. It does not make us pure; only the grace of God can do that. But it completes our lives and fills them out. Heb. 5:9: "Being made perfect, He became the author of eternal salvation unto all them that obey Him." His perfect life and work thus became the source of our salvation. Heb. vi. 1: "Let us go on unto perfection." It is not enough to have entered into His glorious rest, we must fill up the measure of our life. Heb. 7:19: "The law made nothing perfect, but the bringing in of a better hope did." Under the law all men failed. The man who made the law, Moses, was the biggest failure of all. Joshua said, "Ye cannot serve the Lord." Samuel failed as a prophet, David failed as a king, Solomon terribly failed. All under the law failed, for the law made nothing perfect, but the bringing in of a better hope did. God has provided a way for bringing us to perfection, for completing the full will of God in your life and mine. Heb. 7:25: "He is able also to save them to the uttermost that come unto God by Him." Heb. 10:14: "By one offering He hath perfected forever them that are sanctified." There it is at last, Adam could not do it. Moses and Joshua failed. David and Solomon did not perfect it, nor did Elijah, but Jesus Christ did it by one offering. What did He perfect?

1. Our justification. He tells us, Heb. 9:26, that He made an end of sin, and put it away by the sacrifice of Himself. Jesus completely settled for sin. He not only forgives, but obliterates the record forever. In the sacrifices there was a remembrance of sin every year, but

176

He hath put it away. It is again and again emphasized with great power, that He not only forgives sin, but makes an end of it, and the conscience is purged from dead works to serve the living God.

2. Not only perfect cleansing from sin but perfect sanctification to God is provided for. Heb. 10:9, gives the record of it. "Lo, I come to do thy will, oh God." How vain have been our efforts to gain sanctification by our own will or striving. But when His spirit, His will, His life come into us, He who came to do the Father's will, will do it in us. Invite Him to come and He will bring with Him the old voice: "Lo, I come to do thy will." It is the same voice that Paul heard when sinking in despair He cried, "Oh, wretched man that I am." He soon thanked God through Jesus Christ. Christ in him, becoming his life and sanctification, is brought out here as in the other epistles. "By one offering He hath perfected forever them that are sanctified." Beloved, the death and life of Jesus have provided for our sanctification. If you have not got it you are letting go the chief part of salvation. He hath perfected the work and you are letting part of it go by default. Surely this is the meaning of the passage which follows from the prophet Jeremiah. "I will put my law in their hearts." I will make them pure and holy, so that now it will be as easy for them to love as it was to hate, because my very life has been made complete in them. That is Christ's will and covenant for you, to be written in your heart and made perfect in your life.

3. Perfect security. We are to be kept, there is a great deal in Hebrews that is very solemn in the way of warning, a great deal that bids us stand in awe of willful sin. It is like a shining beacon in the sky saying: "If you sin willfully take care; if you do despite to the spirit of God, take care; it is a fearful thing to fall into the hands of the living God. See that ye refuse not Him that speaketh from heaven. Oh, there are solemn words here,

177

but they are put in the midst of such words of cheer. "We are not of them that draw back. One great cable holds in the midst of temptation that comes like a great tempest and hurricane, in the midst of all the slips of our weak, helpless hearts. Both sides are given to us. God is too wise to give us one side only. There are words of awful warning, but there are words of encouragement and cheer also. He does say: "Take care, if you do that you will lose all," but He also says: "I won't fail you." God does give both His warnings and His promises, that the wise Christian may both hope and fear. He has provided a perfect salvation, and He will keep us to the end if we will let Him.

III. – FAITH

The last part of the epistle to the Hebrews is the most comprehensive discussion of faith in the Scriptures. It begins in the early part of the epistle where Israel is spoken of as being led into the Promised Land by faith. In the tenth chapter we are told to cast not away our confidence, which hath great recompense of reward. It is the shield of our spiritual life. The 11th of Hebrews gives us some great examples of faith in Old Testament history, from which we can see many of its different phases. The first is Abel, who teaches us the nature of justifying faith, then Enoch teaches sanctifying faith.

This takes us to Noah who speaks of separating faith. Abraham shows the obedience and test of faith. He went out not knowing whither he went. Isaac shows the patience of faith. In Jacob we see natural meanness overcome through the discipline of faith. Joseph teaches us of the victory of faith over difficulties. These seven characters are a Pleiades indeed. But not one of their number is missing as in that cluster of stars. All are distinct types of faith, and each teaches a different lesson. Then we are told of Moses who through faith brought
178

Israel out of Egypt, and of Joshua who led them into the promised land. These are the two sides of Christian life, deliverance from the world, and entering into God's full inheritance. Later in the chapter is another group of characters which we cannot stop to dwell upon, although each of these also teach a separate lesson of faith. Here are the warriors under Gideon, the prophets under Samuel, the kings under David, the martyrs and women of faith in Old Testament history. This is God's family of faith, and every one of them lived before the Gospel. Don't sit down and say this is glorious, but I can't be like them. God says He has "provided some better thing for us" than even their faith. These are not great mountain peaks like the Himalayas, or Sierras, or Alps, that cannot be climbed. These men lived in the twilight of faith with not half the chance we have. God has provided a better way for us. What is His Provision? "LOOKING UNTO JESUS." Abraham could not do that. Joshua's faith was glorious, but he had not that privilege. What are examples of faith compared with its author. Joshua was not the author of faith, neither was Abraham. And looking at them only makes us feel how different our life is from theirs. But Jesus is the author of our faith. Looking at Jesus does not make me say I wish I had His faith, but He will begin to be in me the same faith. The Old Testament saints were only patterns that dwarf me. The New Testament pattern speaks to me of great faith which is all my own. Jesus does not say to me, "See how high I am, and how low you are," but "See how high I can lift you up." He stoops down and puts His arms around me, and says: "Now steady! steady! trust me, my child!" and then He carries me away up where He is. A child who first tries to write in a copybook does not make his writing look much like the copy, but if the master comes and puts his hand over the child's he can write. Looking at Abraham or Joseph, and merely trying to copy them does not help me much, but looking at Jesus

179

does. If His hand is on mine I can write. Brethren we have more than these men had. It is a shame that we do not take it. Instead of looking at this man or that, God is saying to us, Thou art the man. Beloved do you believe this? Then take Jesus not only as the author, but also as the finisher of your faith, and go on day by day till your Father can say of you with joy, "Behold my beloved Son in whom I am well pleased."

After this there comes another lesson to be learned, and that is the meaning of the discipline and trials, and perplexities that come into the life of faith, and seem to stagger us so, and make the way appear so narrow and so close. Oh! God is wanting to be something to you He has never been before. He is beginning, let Him finish. The last chapter, almost, in this epistle, after that wonderful one about faith, is all about trial and discipline. God tells us in it to faint not nor be discouraged, but endure chastening. Literally this means "child-training" or "schooling." "Now no schooling for the present seemeth to be joyous, but grievous; nevertheless afterwards it yieldeth the peaceable fruit of righteousness to them who are exercised thereby." This kind of work is not pleasant to boys. I well remember when I wanted to be big enough to whip the master, but afterward I came to love him as the greatest benefactor of my early days. In the school of faith we are constantly learning by every day discipline. Then bye-and-bye we shall be taken on the throne. On yonder throne I believe we shall have faith enough to create a world, for we know that by faith they were created. We shall have the faith of God and be able to do as God does. We shall be able to speak to the fig tree and see it wither away. We shall command the mountain to depart and it will go. The day is coming in the millennial world when we shall use faith to do marvelous things. We shall touch the forces of the universe as God touches them. God is training you to have faith for that now. Oh, let Him
180

teach you. Don't be afraid of failing. If the copy gets to be harder, ask Him to put His hand on yours. So looking oft unto Jesus, the author and finisher of faith, go forward, very humbly, for what are we but dust and ashes, but trustfully, for heaven and earth shall pass away before one of His children shall find Him fail. Think not of our weakness but of His faithfulness. Blessed be His holy name He will so keep us until His glorious coming.

CHAPTER XVI.

CHRISTIAN LIFE IN JAMES

"Who is a wise man and endued with knowledge among you? Let him show out of a good conversation his works with meekness of wisdom." – James 3:13.

"The wisdom that is from above is first pure, then peaceable, gentle, and easy to be entreated, full of mercy and good fruits, without partiality, and without hypocrisy. And the fruit of righteousness is sown in peace of them that make peace." – James 3:17-18.

THE FOUR GREAT APOSTLES of the New Testament are types of special phases of Christian character. Paul was the great apostle of faith, John of love, James of practical holiness, and Peter of hope and consolation. His letters teem with tender comfort to the afflicted and distressed. In this quartet James holds a very practical place, and his epistle is a favorite one with minds of this class. It deals with the wholesome, everyday side of life, its trials and temptations, and gives in a very practical form the fruits of Christian living. We have time, this morning, to glance through the epistle only and give its bare outline.

I.

The first aspect of Christian life is given under the word wisdom. In speaking of this, the apostle sums up the practical application of knowledge to life. Knowledge is not wisdom. You have heard of the king who never said a foolish thing and never did a wise one. There are plenty of people who have a great deal of knowledge, but have no idea how to apply it. This was

183

not the case with James. The Holy Ghost came not only to teach, but to guide into all truth – that is, to lead the feet as well as the head, to give not only correct views of the truth of God, but the wisdom also to act it out in the life. This is God's wisdom. It is not enough to believe the Word of God. We must know how to act so as to please God and live out the knowledge we have of Him. Beloved, is your life one of wisdom in this sense?

Now, I think I hear some of the wise people saying: "I told you so. I have no sympathy with these sentimental Christians. I believe in practical common sense, that shines out in words and deeds." James has not a word about that kind of wisdom in his whole epistle. He says: "If any of you lack wisdom let him ask of God, that giveth to all men liberally and upbraideth not, and it shall be given him." It is not natural wisdom he is talking about, not the shrewdness that comes by using one's own reasoning powers, but it is divine wisdom that comes through the spirit. It is Jesus made unto you wisdom. This surely is not natural wisdom. It is the spirit of Jesus living in your heart every day, and showing you how to act. The apostle warns every one who asks for this wisdom to do in faith, nothing wavering, for he that wavereth will receive nothing of God. He received it the same as Paul did through faith. It was the same story of a weak human nature yielded to God, and filled with His wisdom for effective Christian living.

II.

His next view is of practical wisdom in the temptations and trials of life. This is a wisdom that takes you out into the battle, that walks out with you in the midst of distress and persecution, that remains with you when you are surrounded by people who are unjust and false, in the presence of opposing circumstances, in the scorching heat or on the lonely mountain top or passing through the

184

swollen flood; that never forsakes you in any of the trials of life. Have you got this wisdom? "Blessed is the man that endureth temptation; for when he is tried he shall receive the crown of life, which the Lord hath promised to them that love Him." "My brethren, count it all joy when ye fall into divers temptations; knowing this, that the trying of your faith worketh patience. But let patience have her perfect work, that ye may be perfect and entire, lacking nothing." What good is a breastplate that won't stand fire, or a gun that won't go off, or a fortification that won't resist the attack of artillery? If you have got good things in you, you may be sure the devil will test them If you have the right kind of a sword you can go bravely into the battle, and if you have a sword, you will certainly have a battle. If you are willing to endure the trial, you will surely come out from beneath it in victory.

III.

Obedience to God's word. It is not enough to endure temptation, but the word of God must be carried into every day life. We are not to be hearers only but doers. We must go out and obey, working in the perfect law of liberty. "Who so looketh into the perfect law of liberty, and continueth therein he being not a forgetful hearer but a doer of the work this man shall be blessed in his doing," not hearing.

IV.

Practical Christian charity is the next thing. True wisdom and divine charity are always found in the form of love. James gives a very practical picture of this love in the second chapter. It is a picture of the church of God that I wish could be painted by some artist's hand and hung up in every chancel and church of the land. I dare

185

say it would look strange in some of them. Practical Christianity in the epistle of James allows no pew rents, no distinctions of any kind. It does not give the rich man a good seat and send the poor man to a less desirable one further back or off in the gallery. Work of that kind is wrong and ought not to be countenanced by any true Christian. "Hath not God chosen the poor of this world rich in faith and heirs of the kingdom which He hath promised to them that love Him?" "If ye have respect to persons ye commit sin.

Charity in the church means not only this, but it includes a real heart life of love which will control the tongue and restrain the spirit of judgment and criticism. "So speak ye and so do as they that shall be judged by the law of liberty. For he shall have judgment without mercy, that showed no mercy; and mercy rejoiceth against judgment." "Speak not evil one of another, brethren. He that speaketh evil of his brother and judgeth his brother, speaketh evil of the law and judgeth the law; but if thou judge the law thou art not a doer of the law but a judge." If that spirit of love is in the heart it will keep you from condemning or censuring the faults of others. You will be more busy in devising ways to show your love to your brother than in judging him. Oh how this spirit of the devil does get into people, those too that think themselves extremely practical and even spiritual. Many lives have been withered by this horrible spirit of censoriousness taking the place of God on Sinai in judgment and interfering with His sacred rights and prerogatives. The result of it has ever been as James predicted "He shall have judgment without mercy that showed no mercy." There is nothing more sorrowful than to see the working out of this principle. Many have done this thing, but in every case they have turned in at last upon themselves and ended by stinging their own souls. It is not, perhaps, an elegant illustration, but it is an instructive one, the missile that is used in some

186

countries, which describes as ellipse and comes back upon the head of the person who sent it forth. So this sharp judgment and harsh spirit of criticism is sure to come back with crushing force upon the head of the person who indulges in it. The air around is full of these curves, and they play with lightning force upon the persons that hurled the weapon. Judgment is God's business. If you let the missile go it will surely return upon your own head. The scorpion spends its wicked little life in stinging. At last when it has no one else to sting it turns upon its back and stings itself to death. I have seen many a heart broken by its own lack of love and sweetness. It is very solemn to see the man who above all the New Testament characters you might expect to find censorious or critical, James, standing up and says: "Who art thou that judgest another."

V.

In the last part of the second chapter James speaks of practical faith. He places it in a wholesome aspect as something that does, that acts, that steps out and commits itself to some test. If you believe God you can venture on Him. You will not be afraid to risk a great deal. Faith acts. If a sick man believes he is well, he will not remain in bed, but he will get up and walk. So in every case real faith does not wait until the mountain has disappeared, but it goes on and walks over it. God grants us all the faith that shows itself by its works, and proves to all men the difference between the work of faith and the works of unbelief."

VI.

Practical control of the tongue is the next theme in this epistle. James makes more of this than of anything else. He says it is the test of holiness and even of conversion.

He says if any man seem to be religious, or ritualistic, for the word means ritualism, if any man *seem* to be religious and bridleth not his tongue, he does not amount to anything. His talk is nothing but a jingle and a rattle. "If any man offend not in word, the same is a perfect man." A man who can hold his tongue can do anything in Christian life. But the man who cannot control his tongue is a poor empty thing. There is no stamina in him. More than that there is something in him that is capable of doing very terrible work. There is a volcano there that may burst out any moment into a Charleston earthquake. "The tongue is a fire, a world of iniquity; so is the tongue among our members, that it defileth the whole body, and setteth on fire the course of nature; and it is set on fire of hell." A man may be able to tame all kinds of wild beasts, but he cannot tame the tongue. He may tame the fierce hawk and kite, and even more ferocious birds, but he cannot tame the tongue. Many of the venomous serpents, even the cobra and boa can be handled by their keepers in safety, but the tongue cannot be controlled. The inhabitants of the sea, the crocodile and alligator can be tamed, and even fishes can be taught some things, but the tongue can no man tame. It is not only used in blasphemy against the Lord, but men and women will sing God's praises together in His holy temple, and before they leave the precincts of the sacred place, give themselves up to words of malignity and, perhaps, close the day with some false atrocious slander. Oh, friends, well may James say this is a thing that is set on fire of hell. We should fear it in ourselves and shun it in others as we would a rabid dog, or a plague ship in the harbor which is not allowed to land, but compelled to remain in quarantine alone. Dear friends, strive for a practical control of your words. It is the real test of victory for you and for me. You will lose more by one-half uttered sentence of criticism than you will gain by many words for God. You never came to the time when

188

you were reproved by God for being too silent. You cannot be a holy Christian, a truly humble child of God, unless you know His gentleness, who walked the earth, the meek and lowly One, without one word of unloving criticism or censure. "This wisdom descendeth not from above, but is earthly, sensual, devilish." May the Holy Ghost complete in us today what he began on the day of Pentecost when there came such a baptism of fire upon the disciples resting upon them as cloven tongues. Before Isaiah could go out to serve the Lord, his tongue had to be touched with fire, and when Job became really conscious of God's presence the effect was to bow him down in the dust and make him hold his tongue in silence. So upon us may the baptism of fire descend as cloven tongues, filling us with the spirit of Divine love, and burning out of us this filthiness of our unsanctified tongue.

VII.

Practical separation from the world, James 4:1-4. James says the world is God's enemy, and if we give it the heart we are faithless to God as Israel was of old. If we find pleasure in the world we are finding it with His enemies. But the spirit that dwelleth in us loveth to jealousy." That is the Holy Spirit loves to jealousy. He wants us wholly for Jesus. He wants us to love Him entirely, and give Him the first and best affection and devotion of our hearts. If the world shares these we have the spirit of adulterers and adulteresses, and cannot offer to God that which is holy. The world cannot touch without defiling. We must be separate, we must come out from the world, and its sinful pleasure and desires. "Go to now, ye rich men, weep and howl for your miseries that shall come upon you. Your riches are corrupted, and your garments are moth eaten. Your gold and silver is cankered; and the rest of them shall be a

189

witness against you, and shall eat your flesh as it were fire. Ye have heaped treasure together for the last days." But ye, brethren, who have left to His judgment, who have turned your back upon it and are living only for God, "be patient unto the coming of the Lord."

VIII.

Finally, James speaks of the practical ministry of prayer and faith. James 5:13-20. He advises prayer for the afflicted, praise for the joyful, and prayer for the sick. That is practical surely. Are you in trouble, pray about it. Are you very happy, praise the Lord. Are you sick, pray. This is the lever that lifts real loads, and the hands of prayer are the hands that reach real needs. Pray for others. So shall you move the hand that can touch the people you love. This is the force that restrains from sin and suffering, the arm that reaches the world, the power that conquers the stronghold of Satan, that withers the fig tree of sin, and takes hold of the throne for victory in daily life. Oh, mighty ministry of prayer. Oh wondrous power that can touch the spirits around the throne and send them forth, like the houses Zechariah saw, to quiet the air in the north country. Prayer will go where you cannot go. It will open doors you cannot open. It will touch the arm that moves the universe. Think of the glorious spirit of prayer that dwelt in the frail body of Elijah, who was weak enough to fly from a woman and almost wreck the work he had begun to do for God. James says: "Elias was a man subject to like passions as we are, and he prayed." He lived in an age of the world when there was no one to cheer him on in his work. He was sent from the lone hills of Gilead to cry out against the wickedness of Israel. There was no human arm to help him on. He worked alone and singlehanded. His bold spirit did not shrink from its task till the whole nation cried out "The Lord, He is God!" Israel was
190

saved from wreck in answer to his prayer. He prayed again, with his head between his knees in a sort of wrestling agony, and continued it till in the sky a little cloud appeared and the large drought of three years was over. The ministry of Elijah was a glorious victory of faith. He said very little, but alone with God he did a great deal. God is weary of our fears. He has given us a mighty force, and he is waiting to do great things for us. He has blessings to pour in upon us. He would fill us with His own holy will. But we need to make up and lay hold with strong faith on this mighty power which can touch all heaven and fill all earth with risk of fire. We read in Revelation that there was silence in Heaven for half an hour. Why was it? In that time there was going up the incense of the prayers of the saints and all heaven was still. God said, "Hush! my people are praying." And all heaven stood still till the golden bowl of incense was carried up by the hands of Jesus, and then came a mighty change. An angel laid a coal of fire upon the incense and poured it out upon the earth, and immediately there were voices, and thunderings, and lightnings, and an earthquake. All the powers of nature and providence began to move to answer prayer. Such is the ministry of prayer. It ascends up to heaven, and then is poured back upon us in mighty power. Our Lord will undoubtedly come in days of like Elijah's, which were days of great prayer. God is only waiting for the last words of the epistle of James to be fulfilled before ushering in the end of the age. It has already begun to be fulfilled in the healing of the sick and the comfort of the sorrowing. We have not seen it fully yet. There are three kinds of prayer spoken of in James, for the afflicted, for the sick, and for the lost. We have not made as much of the last as of the others. Let us begin this day to prove the power of these closing words. "He which converteth the sinner from the error of his way shall save a soul from death, and shall hide a multitude of sins."

191

CHAPTER XVII.

CHRISTIAN LIFE IN FIRST PETER

"But the God of all grace, who hath called me unto His eternal glory by Christ Jesus, after that ye have suffered a while, make you perfect, stablish, strengthen, settle you. To Him be glory and dominion for ever and ever. Amen." – 1Pet. 5:10-11.

WHEN THE DEAR LORD looked into Peter's future, telling him how all the powers of hell should try to sift him as wheat, and that only the power of Christ could save him, He told him the time would come when he should look back on all this great trial, having become firmly established, his feet settled on the solid rock, stronger for the testing and his shameful fall, and that his ministry then would be to strengthen his brethren. "When thou art converted," He said, "strengthen thy brethren." Peter himself said afterward: "I will not be negligent to put you always in remembrance of these things." His life was one constant endeavor to comfort and strengthen. These two letters were written as a part of the fulfillment of his Master's charge. They were intended to comfort, strengthen and cheer the suffering children of God. They were written just before the fearful tempest that resulted in the martyrdom of himself and Paul. Probably when the letters reached their destination Rome was in flames, with Nero gloating in his palace over the ruin he had caused that he might rebuild the city in marble and gold, and make it more splendid than ancient Babylon. Then he circulated the rumor that it had been done by the Christians. It was enough to breathe the thought of evil to make it quickly circulate. A grain of wheat grows slowly, but the thistle-down flies on the wings of the wind. There went forth a storm of indignation against the children of God. It was vain to reply against the slander. There followed a time of fearful persecution, and it was not long before Peter and Paul both fell before it. These letters were written just before it came. They were sent to prepare the way for the fiery trial that was to come. Their one theme is consolation in the midst of suffering and trial of every kind. Their keynote is hope and comfort sounding above the minor note of sorrow. It takes two notes to make a chord. So here are the two notes of hope and suffering, the one above the other.

The two verses of our text form a perfect table of contents of the whole letter. There is to be glory beyond this life, and there is to be suffering here. But through the suffering is to come something better than glory. We are to be established, strengthened, settled. The suffering will be intense for a time. But it will result in our being settled forever on the solid rock, where sorrow and trial will come no more or if they come, be powerless to move us.

Let us look a little more closely at the letter penned by this dear old apostle, and study the lessons he learned in the ordeal of affliction.

I.

The first thing we find in the letter is a bright picture of hope and promise, Peter begins just where God would have us begin. It is away up yonder. Before he lets us look at the lurid fire or fear the flame, he bids us look up, and then he paints the picture of an inheritance incorruptible, undefiled and that fadeth not away. He knows we cannot go through the earthly pathway unless we have seen the glorious prize beyond.

"Blessed be the God and Father of our Lord Jesus Christ which according to His abundant mercy hath
194

begotten us again unto a lively hope by the resurrection of Jesus Christ from the dead to an inheritance incorruptible and undefiled, and that fadeth not away, reserved in heaven for you, who are kept by the power of God through faith unto salvation ready to be revealed in the last time." – 1Pet. 1:3-5.

That is the place to begin. The way to get ready for trial is to look up. A sea-captain once sent his boy up into the rigging of the ship, and as he began to look down into the dizzy depth below him and tremble, the father shouted to him: "Look up." The child obeyed him and went on in safety. So Peter says to you, beloved, look up; yonder is the prize. The trials here are not worth looking at. There is the incorruptible inheritance. Keep your heart fixed on things above. That is the way to overcome trouble. Jesus Himself would have succumbed if he had looked down. I have sometimes wondered if that is the reason why just before the cross He said not a word about his own trial. He told His disciples: "In the world *ye* shall have tribulation," but He said not a word about His own terrible trial that was so near. "He endured the cross, despising the shame." He looked through it and saw the glory of the throne beyond, and the rest and joy laid up there for Him and for us. Oh, beloved, keep your eye upon the heavenlies. Think of the mansions yonder. The disciples were able to take joyfully the spoiling of their goods, knowing there was something infinitely better awaiting them. What if you lost fifteen thousand dollars last week, you have not lost that inheritance. What if you should lose twenty thousand next week, you are richer then than Jesus was. You talk about trials here, there it will be; "I will confess your name before my Father." You think people do not understand you here, there "the righteous shall shine forth as the sun in the kingdom of their Father." For He hath promised to bring forth thy righteousness as the light and thy judgment as the noonday. What though you

195

have been full of pains and aches here, the body won't know what pain means there; it will forget how it feels to be sick. What though scalding tears have flowed down your face here, His own hand shall wipe them away forevermore, and every tear shall become a jewel in your crown if they were shed for Jesus, Look up! Look up! I am so glad Peter hangs the crown in the sky, and bids us look beyond the cross. There is real comfort in this for you and me. Let us keep our eye upon it and lose sight of the trial.

II.

"Wherein ye greatly rejoice, though now for a season if need be ye are in heaviness through manifold temptations: that the trial of your faith, being much more precious than of gold that perisheth, though it be tried with fire, might be found unto praise and honor and glory at the appearing of Jesus Christ." – 1Pet. 1:6-7.

That is the other side of the picture, the dark shade in it. Peter speaks of manifold temptations. They do not come to us once only, but two, three, four times, and just as you think surely now you have been tried enough and have learned to triumph, they keep coming. You thought last year was trying, but this summer has been more so, and this autumn has opened up as no other has, full of deep trial. That is just what Peter said would happen. We are to meet manifold temptations. They will keep coming and coming and coming. Don't you find that is the way? Ah! you would not like to miss any of them if there is a "need be" for them, and there surely is as long as they come. They will come from every direction. Temptations directly from the devil; temptations from the world; temptations from the men and women around you, even those who are closest at your side; temptations from your own heart; temptations from the circumstances in which you are placed. They are manifold, so that you often feel like saying: "I have the hardest life any one ever had; I have to meet more difficulties than any other Christian ever did. "Why have I such a hard time when he or she has such an easy one?" You forget that "there hath no temptation taken you but such as is common to man." You did not really believe that after all; you thought you had a little monopoly in the matter of trials. "God is faithful, who will not suffer you to be tempted above that you are able, but will with the temptation also make a way to escape, that ye may be able to bear it." Do you believe that? I am afraid not. Peter says the same afflictions are accomplished in your brethren that are in the world. There is a little conceit often about the way people look at their lives. It savors a little of impertinence for you to think your life is the hardest one in the world. My life is just as hard as yours; yours is just as hard as mine. They are different, but they are equally trying. God has said so.

Again, the trial is to be a fiery trial, and the same one is not often repeated. It will be "a strange thing" next time. When we have been tested in one direction and know how to stand there, that kind of temptation does not come again. God knows better than to set his child the same copy to write over again. The apostle tells us to think it not strange concerning the fiery trial which is to try you. The same trial will never be quite the same. It will burn a little deeper next time. The colors will be brought out clearer and richer.

Peter uses another word which enhances the suffering: "*Ye are in heaviness* through manifold temptations." If the trial does not press the heart down we need not mind it. But an old log that has remained in the water a long time gets water-logged and heavy. And so it sometimes happens that long-continued trial may make a Christian heavy too. He is apt to lose spring a little and not rebound from pressure as of old. A cloud does sometimes come over the spirit and the trouble is not met

197

with the same buoyancy that it used to be. There is a heaviness from manifold temptations. A friend said to me this summer he had heard many Christians say that they were full of joy all the time, but it had been his experience that whenever a real trial came to him it always cut deeply. It went home to his heart, and for a time, perhaps, depressed him, although he never gave up faith for a moment. It did produce heart-heaviness. Paul says: "No chastening for the present seemeth to be joyous, but grievous; nevertheless afterward it yieldeth the peaceable fruit of righteousness." It is all right, brother. Jesus felt so too. "My soul is exceeding sorrowful, even unto death." Trial will scorch everything it touches. But though we may be in heaviness we should never become doubtful, or peevish, or morbid. We should never let the light get off our faces. We should let the Lord know of the heaviness and get the victory there, and then come out from it stronger to help others. The clouds should bring rain, else there is no good in their coming.

III.

Let us now look a little at the bright side. There is always a "need be" for every trial. It would not come unless there was a necessity for it. God knows what is required, and He lets it come into the life. He ordered it wisely, for He is teaching His child. He knows when to send it and how long to let it stay.

Again, it is only for a little while, "for a season." Peter says: God will not let it always last, if it did it would burn up everything. He shortens the day.

Then too the trial is very "precious" to God. He looks at it with deep solicitude. He stands as a jeweler does over a crucible; careful that the fire does not burn too long; or as a housewife over her dinner, which will be spoiled with too much cooking. God knows when the work is done; trust Him. The work He is doing is very precious. While we are scolding and fretting about it, we are missing the lessons. He smites in wisdom and love.

IV.

1. Our armor for the trial is, first, practical holiness and a blameless life in communion with God, and faithful obedience to His holy will. "Be ye holy," runs all through the first three chapters of this epistle. Peter dwells on this great theme which has been the subject of so many other letters, and urges to a holy consecrated life, hid with Christ in God. His first picture is the same as that given in the other epistles, the holiness of God. "Be ye holy, for I am holy." Then he speaks of the purified souls of believers. Again, we are to show forth the praises of Him who hath called us out of darkness into His marvelous light. Then he brings down sanctification to daily life and beseeches the saints, as strangers and pilgrims, to abstain from fleshly lusts that war against the soul. Next their duty to those around is pointed out; they are told to honor all men, that is show no disrespect to any. Wives are advised to be loving, gentle, modest, deferential, holy; husbands to be loving, faithful, tender and true. All are told to eschew evil and do good. If any suffer for righteousness' sake, or are believed to be unrighteous, they are not to be afraid or troubled, but bear it so that their accusers shall be ashamed in the day when their true character is known.

What is the secret of this holiness? It comes from union with Christ. "As newborn babes desire the sincere milk of the word that ye may grow thereby." This is not natural holiness. It is God's spirit and life born in you. Again, the 4th chapter speaks of our being cleansed from sin, dead in Christ and risen in Him, as Christ suffered in the flesh so we are to suffer and die with Him. And as Christ rose from the dead, so we are to live according to

199

God in the spirit. No life can be holy till the divine life is formed within it.

2. Our armor is also to be simple trust and confidence in God's power and love and care. Let them who suffer, commit the keeping of their souls to Him. Commit means to hand over, to trust wholly to another. So if we give our trials to Him He will carry them. If we walk in righteousness He will carry us through. The same spirit appears in the 5th chapter. Humble yourselves therefore under the mighty hand of God that He may exalt you in due time. There are two hands there, God's hand pressing us down, humbling us, and then God's hand lifting us up; cast all you care on Him, then His hand will lift you up, exalt you in due time. There are two cares in this verse, your care and His care. They are different in the original. One means anxious care, the other means almighty care. Cast your anxious care on Him and take His almighty care instead. Take no account of trouble any more, but believe He is able to sustain you through it. The government is on His shoulder. Believe *that*, if you know what trouble is, and you shall also know of walking through it with humble, holy heart, in blessed deliverance. This will make you right with every human being, so that you can look in every face and in His face and say, "All is right! "You will be casting, casting, always as every new care comes. If you do not do this, you will not be delivered. If you fret and worry, God will let you do it, and stand off till you can give the matter to Him. If you are overcome, one or the other of these things is true, you do not believe He cares, or you are not casting your care on Him. It is just like the disciples of old. "Master carest thou not that we perish." If your child should say that to you, you would feel deeply wronged. How must God feel to have His children say so to Him? Oh, friends trust Him, He *does* care; He sometimes lets the trial be very hard, and come very near to the disciples, so that no earthly power can
200

help. He lets it go on till He sees if we are going to let Him manage it. He sometimes will even let help come in, that is not His care, to see if we will take it. He does test to see if we are truly trusting Him. If we are, there is glorious deliverance. God lets the pressure come in a thousand ways as heavy as it could be borne, but He gives the trust, and He sets His seal upon the trust so gloriously. It is not easy naturally to trust in this way. It is trusting in the dark, and sometimes, in it one is almost baffled and overcome. It seems so impossible that this should be made right. But God does it and how much stronger we are for the conflict, and how sweet the trust with which we can look up to heaven at last, and say, "Thou hast done it Father, thou didst come." If Jesus sends the little ship across the stormy lake He will surely come to it upon the water. He will not fail His trusting child, who went because He said "Go!" The disciples went at His bidding and He carried them through. One reason why God lets us be so tried is to make our trust firmer, to make us know from personal experience, that in the Lord Jehovah is everlasting strength.

V.

Peter speaks also of the glorious spiritual result of trial, that is to establish, strengthen, and settle the believer. When I was a little fellow they set me to pounding the earth down with a mallet around some posts where the men were putting up a fence, and I wondered why they did not shovel the dirt in all at once and have it done with. Oh, they knew the fence would not stand a good blow if the earth was not packed around it. It needs heavy weight there to make it solid. When God makes a fence, when He plants you as a pillar in His temple He too wants the ground packed down around you so you will stand firm when trial comes. You would not get your cook to take an easy way to make bread, would

201

you? You wouldn't tell her to hurry up and not stop to knead it so much, would you? I am afraid you would be in a hurry too at the table. Good bread must be well kneaded, and so must good Christians. Diamonds are not valued so much for their size as for the number of cuttings or facets there are on them. So with God's children. God keeps cutting them down again and again, till sometimes you almost think the stone will be gone, but they come out many sided reflecting the brightness of the sun from every angle. This is God's purpose – and only suffering came to make room for it. If you get in a tight place don't try to wriggle through it. God can manage that matter as well as He can your salvation. He wishes to make you perfect, then establish you, that is, make you solid. Many Christians are not solid. They catch impressions very soon, but they lose them very soon also. Then God lets them suffer. He puts them through the school of discipline, and the lessons they learn there they do not forget. I don't profess to have suffered more than you, but nothing ever has brought me so near God, or emptied me so that Christ could fill me. And I never have passed through such a season of trial that I have not been able afterward to help some one that I could not have reached before. This discipline will strengthen you; it will make more of you until at last you shall be settled to be moved no more. You shall become so rooted in God, so fixed on the eternal rock that you can say with Paul, "None of these things move me." There is a difference between being moved and uprooted. The little sapling may be moved by the wind; the great oak cannot be moved. So I suppose you have been through some trials that have moved you more than others, but if you have been moved at all you are not quite settled. You are like the sapling and not like the oak. God wants us not only to stand, but to stand immovably. So we can say as did David in the 46th Psalm, God is in the midst of her, she shall not be moved.
202

We shall indeed feel the full severity of the shock, but we are not anxious about it, for God has all the responsibility. Therefore awake the song of trust now in the midst of the trial. Glorify God in the fire. Travelers tell us of a plant in Africa that never blossoms in fine weather. It is a poor common looking thing, but let the hot wind of the desert, the fearful sirocco begin to blow, and the little, rugged, ugly plant opens its petals, and is transformed into a thing of bloom and beauty. I don't know why it is, but it is a fact that it blossoms in a tempest. Oh! to be able to blossom in the tempest. Beloved, when this life is all over, how we will wish we had done so. We never shall be able to do it again, we can never overcome the devil another time, never have an opportunity of showing what Christ can do through us any more. Won't we be almost sorry we cannot win another crown? Let us stand in these precious hours that will so soon be gone. The old man that wrote this epistle had been in the struggle many, many years, he had seen all sides of life, and I am sure he spoke the truth. The conflict must be entered on here, but there is glory yonder at the appearing of Jesus Christ; "To Him be glory and dominion forever and ever, Amen."

CHAPTER XVIII

CHRISTIAN LIFE IN SECOND PETER THE INFINITE RESOURCES OF GRACE.

"His divine power Hath given unto us all things that pertain unto life and godliness, through the knowledge of him that hath called us to glory and virtue," or "by His glory and virtue." (See margin.) – 2Pet. 1:3.

---

*T*HE FIRST EPISTLE OF PETER, we saw last Sabbath morning is the Epistle of Consolation and of Hope, addressed to God's afflicted children and containing the richest comfort amid the testings and trials of life, and the secret of those mysteries which have so oft perplexed His people, but which are so plain in the light of His loving discipline. This second Epistle is the epistle of the coming and the kingdom of our Lord Jesus Christ, and in these opening verses, before he proceeds to speak about that blessed hope, he tells us how we may be prepared to obtain an abundant entrance into the everlasting kingdom of our Lord and Saviour Jesus Christ. And in the tenth verse, as he closes this wonderful paragraph in the opening of the chapter: "If these things be in you and abound, they shall make you that ye shall be neither barren nor unfruitful in the knowledge of our Lord and Saviour Jesus Christ. Wherefore, give diligence to make your calling and election sure, for if you do these things ye shall never fall or stumble, for so an entrance shall be ministered unto you abundantly into the everlasting kingdom of our Lord and Saviour Jesus Christ."

These verses, then, that fill up the first part of this chapter describe the enrobement and preparation which we need in order to obtain an entrance abundantly into the everlasting kingdom of our Lord and Saviour Jesus Christ. As in the First Epistle that glorious kingdom was the pole-star of hope and comfort, an inheritance incorruptible, undefiled and that fadeth not away, was the starting point of Peter as he comforted God's suffering children; so in this epistle it is the culminating point. It is the glorious goal to which the Church is moving on, and where Christian faith and hope at last will find a glad consummation. But while it is a blessed hope and a near hope, it is a very solemn hope; and he that hath this hope in him purifieth himself even as He is pure; and it needs that we shall prepare to meet Him, and that we shall hear the voice which says: "Behold the bridegroom cometh, go ye out to meet him." " Blessed is he that watcheth and keepeth his garments, lest he walk naked and they see his shame." "The marriage of the Lamb has come and His wife has made herself ready, and it was granted to her that she should be arrayed in fine raiment, clean and white." That is the raiment which these verses so gloriously describe, and I know not of any other passage in the whole New Testament so overladen with deep spiritual truth as this wonderful paragraph. Let us, then, with grave and thoughtful attention, as Christians that want the substantial and solid meat of God's Holy Word, let us ask the spirit of God to show it to us, and then to give it to us, bringing it into our spirit, and into our heart, as our living bread and our daily experience and strength.

I.

First, we have God's calling and election; what God has called us to, and what God has called us from. Having escaped the corruption that is in the world through lust, He hath called you to glory and virtue; give all diligence to make your calling and your election sure. He has called us from the corruption of the world
206

through lust, called us to the glory and virtue that has come of His own character. The language used here is taken from the description of Lot's escape from Sodom, "having escaped," the Greek verb carries with it the force of having fled in terror, having been hastily and narrowly delivered from corruption; and the word corruption there, in the original carries with it the force of destruction, having fled in terror from the destruction of the world through the force of lust, the lust of evil things, the carnal heart; not the world that God made, which would never hurt us, but the lust of the world, the fire that takes hold of the world and burns us up with unhallowed flame, the lust of the flesh, the lust of the eyes, the pride of life, the trinity of devilishness and fleshliness and earthliness, and corruption, which is the natural God of every human heart. We have escaped it, we have fled from it, we have been narrowly delivered from it; we were lost in its arms, but we have turned our backs upon it and put our fingers in our ears, and burst forth with the cry, "Life, eternal life." And now before us is the other prospect: He has called us to glory and virtue, not lust, but virtue; not the world, but glory. Called us to glory and to virtue. Now I believe we are to find the meaning of these words "calling" and "election" in connection with this thought. I believe that God has set before each of us a prize as His redeemed children, and that the idea running through this passage all the way in connection with our calling and election is the winning of this prize. God has called you to a prize, a glorious prize, to a prize of virtue, to a prize of righteousness and purity and grandeur, and eternal magnificence in His everlasting kingdom. And now you have got to make your calling and election sure. You have got to answer the call, and see that you do not lose the election. You are a candidate for it, but you might lose the election. I do not think the word election has any reference at all to the bare question of our salvation, but it has reference after we are saved to the question

207

whether we shall win the prize or not, whether we shall gain the crown or not; we are all candidates, but one receiveth the prize. I do believe, therefore, this word refers to the successful competitor in the Christian race, and that for you and me the message is, while we have all been pardoned through the blood of Christ, we are not all going to make our calling and election sure. That is, we are not all going to gain an abundant entrance into His kingdom, but only he that overcomes shall inherit all things. God gives us all a place in His mercy, and then He has said, yonder are the prizes; blessed is the man that overcomes, he shall win. Can ye drink of My cup; are ye able to sit on My right hand and on My left. If ye are ye shall be elected to that position of honor and glory. Election always implies this thought, special honor, special position, special favor and dignity, and now beloved you are candidates for a crown. Your election depends more on your own vote than anybody else's. Give all diligence that ye make it sure. God has called you to glory and to virtue. Dare you be content any more with an unholy profession and with a defeated life?

II.

Now then, secondly, and in the next place, God has great resources for this Christian life; that is the glorious call; you have all got it. If you have not, it has come to you today. God calls you out of Sodom. Lot was a Christian, but he was in Sodom and Gomorrah. Abraham was called out of Sodom, and he heard the call. You may be a Christian, and not have heard God's call to holiness. God has called us to holiness; God has called us to glory. God has called us to a prize and a kingdom. Now then, He gives us resources for it. His divine power has granted to us all things that pertain to life and godliness. He has not called you to go on your own resources but He has provided all that is necessary, beloved, for your claiming this eternal glory. His divine power has given to us all things that pertain to life and godliness. There is no place here for whining over your inability, and your temptations. His divine power has given us all things that are necessary for life and godliness. For life, that is eternal life; godliness, that is a holy life, a life of entire consecration. God has provided resources for every Christian living such a life. God's omnipotence has provided all things necessary to life and godliness. Must He repeat it until it gets written on our stubborn hearts? How we doubt it, and disbelieve it, and march around it, and evade it, but God says there is a provision for life and godliness abundant for everybody, and His omnipotence has given all the resources which you require for a true Christian life, and for a godly, consecrated, victorious existence, till your crown is won. Beloved, do you believe it? That God gives you this morning panoply enough for the battle, provision enough for the march, and equipment enough for every possible situation in which you ever can be placed. If that is so, there is no excuse for anybody living a life of unholiness; if that be so, it is obligatory upon us to live such a life; if that be so, it is criminal in us not to lead it, it is inexcusable in us not to lead it. It is neglecting the great salvation not to take it. Christian friends, this morning do you honestly believe that God's divine power has provided for us all things that pertain to life and godliness?

III.

Again, in the next place we see the solid ground of this provision, through the righteousness of Jesus Christ, our Saviour. This provision is secured to us by the righteousness of Christ. It is bought for us, it is paid for us, it is purchased for us, and it belongs to us. It is our right through Jesus Christ, to have all things that pertain to life and godliness. Into yonder armory our captain has gone and bought an outfit, and the best outfit that Heaven can provide for every one of us. Like the traveler going off to some far land, and wanting thousands for his journey's preparation, and wondering how he is going to get the means. A friend comes and deposits thousands of dollars and says, "Go and get everything you need. Do you need changes of raiment, provisions and food? Do you need a house to live in, a boat in which to navigate the waters, a company of helpers and servants to go along with you? It is all provided; go and draw to the utmost extent of my deposit." Oh, the Lord Jesus has provided for us an outfit for our journey, an outfit for our march, an outfit for our victory, everything we can ever need, daily strength, daily comfort, daily light, daily victory, complete triumph, and on to the crown. He has provided it through His righteousness. You are entitled to it, and if you do not get it, you are getting less than your right. And you can go to God and claim the grace of holiness, as one of your redemption rights. You can go to God, and claim the precious faith of this chapter as one of your redemption rights. You can go to God, and claim the strength you need as one of Christ's redemption purchases. You can go and claim that Satan shall be bruised under your feet, as bought for you by the redemption and righteousness of Christ. How comfortable we feel, when we know we are entitled by right to a thing; so this comes through the righteousness of our Lord and Saviour, even Jesus Christ.

IV.

Next there are the title deeds, "whereby are given to us exceeding great and precious promises." That is how this divine provision comes to us. It comes to us through a series of papers and title-deeds so numerous, so varied, and so surpassing our highest thought or need, that he
210

just looks at the bundle of papers and he says, "Here are the title-deeds of my inheritance; I cannot count them." When men give you a farm or a house, or a piece of valuable property, they give you but one deed. But when God gives all things that pertain to life and holiness, he gives you this mass of title-deeds and papers, that we have bound up in pages and called our Bible.

We might call it our check-book, with ten thousand times ten thousand checks, endorsed by the name of God's dear Son, and payable on presentation and delivery; exceeding great and precious promises, and every one of them is good for the help you need at any moment of your Christian life. When he speaks about them, he gets overwhelmed, they are so precious. He speaks of the precious blood of Christ, the precious trial of faith, and here of the precious promises. Precious, like the things that men go and seek for in mines, and in the bottom of the sea, gold and gems, and rare things. God's promises are scattered, not like hidden grains of gold, but lavished as the sands beneath our feet, and as the stars above our gaze; thousands and tens of thousands; so many that no man has ever counted them all. Some tell us there are twenty thousand, some tell us there are forty thousand; I do not know how many, but they are exceeding great. Exceeding, that means beyond measurement; exceeding your ideas, your thoughts, your expectations, your need, your weakness, your trials. They always overlap it, and go beyond it; they are exceeding great. They are higher than the highest place where God bids you stand. They are deeper than the lowest abasement of suffering and trial. They are broader than "the widest possible need of life. They are stronger than your weakness, or your greatest need of strength. They are always exceeding great, transcending all that you are able either to ask or to think. Now, these promises of God's are God's title-papers, His deeds of possession through which we come into these great

211

provisions He has made for our Christian life, so that if you want to get anything from God, you must take the promise and claim it, and count it yours, and then in answer to every case there comes correspondent blessing. God expects you to take the promises and use them as you use a bank check; just discount them, turn them into actual currency; turn them into real value; use them at the critical moments of life, and I am sure you will find everyone of them overlap your need, and you will say they are exceedingly great and precious, and through them you have all things that pertain to life and godliness.

V.

Now once more he tells us the very substance and essence of this divine provision that thus comes to us, and thus he leads us to a higher thought even than any we have yet reached, he says that by these promises we may be partakers of God's gifts? No. Of God's works of Creation? No. Of God's spiritual help? No. BUT OF THE DIVINE NATURE — OF GOD HIMSELF. The provision then that God has made for life and godliness is nothing less than God's own nature, God's own nature, and makes us as efficient and sufficient for the need as God Himself is sufficient. Oh, this is wonderful, beloved. I am not able to understand it as I would this morning, and as I would have you understand it, but it does seem so marvelous, that instead of giving us help He gives us Himself; instead of sending us power He puts His own omnipotence in our breast, and puts His own nature in our nature, and makes us part of the Deity, part of God, partners of His infinite all-sufficiency through the great and precious promises. Now that is the great point to which the ages have been trying to reach. As we read the ancient religions, we find that all were trying somehow to get God and man into partnership. We find them
212

cutting out of stones their ideals and conceptions of uniting God to man, putting God in human forms, and yet, alas, putting human lusts in God Himself. But they all failed, because they could not understand God's holiness. It was God brought down to the level of man, and not man brought up to the level of God. But oh, through God's incarnate Son, through Jesus, man hath in him all the fullness of the Godhead bodily. Through Jesus we are brought up to God's very bosom, and nature and life and fellowship, and not only seated with Him on the throne, but the heart of God is put into our heart, and the very nature of God into our being. So that it is natural for us to feel as God feels; it is natural for us to do as God does; it is second nature as God's is. That is the consummation of Christian life and character. This is not a man walking up the steps of Christian virtue, but it is God coming into a man, and putting into him His own being and holiness, and spiritual beauty and grandeur. Brethren, I feel so humbled before this. I see it afar off as when I have looked upon a mountain of ice in its white-robed majesty, and somehow I couldn't get my arms around it, or get up its cliffs or sides, or get a picture of it that brought it all into the range of a single view, so it seems to me this colossal thought of God, coming into us, and making us partakers of the divine nature is so vast, and yet it is so simple and so hopeful, that I would fain have you know it, and yet I despair myself of ever perfectly or fully being able to realize it or to describe it. But I think you will understand enough of it to see how much greater it is than anything man could ever do or be. You know what nature is. When you see a thistle growing up with sharp spear points, and sending its nasty roots into your garden soil, and piercing you as you grasp it and try to look at its blossom, you say, well, the thing is according to its nature. When you see the thorn-bush, raising thorns, you never expect it to raise apples, for you say, it is its nature to be a thorn. When

213

you see a fish floating in the water, and in vain trying to live upon the shore, or mount into the air, you say it is its nature, it is according to its nature to live that way. When you see a little bird mounting up with light wings, and letting the air be its chariot, you say, it is its nature to fly and to float, and to live such a life. You cannot make it do anything else. You cannot make it live in the sea, any more than you can make the fish live in the air. Both of them live according to their nature. When you put the nature of a bird into a bird, it cannot help flying. When you put the nature of a lower order of creation into it, it grovels like a hog in the mire and wallows according to its nature. The only way to get it out is to put a new nature in it. So that when men want to improve the quality of their fruit, they put in a new graft and then it grows spontaneously. That is just what we want. Men are taking human nature and trying to make it holy, but they cannot, for it is not in humanity. The only way is to bring God's nature in, and then it will be like the heart and the body of the bird put into the groveling worm. It will go out because it is its nature. And so God does not take a whip and lash you, and say you must fly. It would be cruel to go to the swine and beat him because he grovels, and say, get up and sit on the branches and sing with the lark. He would grunt back to you his helplessness and despair, and the more you beat him the more helpless would he be. God does not come to man and say, you must do this, and you must feel that; but He comes to them and says, let Me transform your nature, let Me put My heart into your faintness, and My life into your death, and My love into your selfishness. Naturally man does wrong; he cannot help it. He knows he does it, and if he is an honest man, he will say I cannot help it. I do wrong and I cannot help it. He is earthly, and if he is candid, and if he tells you the truth, he will say, I love the world, and do find pleasure in these things, and I cannot help it. That is true, and you will find honest men that do

214

it. But only let God's new nature get into that man, and then the man will rouse himself just as naturally as that corpse would rise that you are trying to carry. It takes four men to carry a dead man, and then it is hard work. But let life come into that man, and no man needs carry him, because there is life in him; and so God does not want to carry you as a corpse, but wants to put the loving heart of God into you, and then you will rise and walk, and then just live the life of God. And so He says His great purpose is to unite us to Him by His promises and by His Holy Spirit, and bring down into these vessels of clay, the nature of the living God, put His law into our heart, and His holiness into our being, and His faith in the midst of our feebleness, and His love in the midst of our selfishness, and His purity in the midst of our sin, and just lift us up by the self-moving power of God's own nature in us. Beloved, that is God's provision for life and godliness, and He brings it to you and to me.

VI.

There is still one more link in this great passage without which all the rest would fail. How are we going to rise into this divine life, and thus be prepared for all things necessary for life and godliness? It is but one little word, one essential link, without which all the rest were vain. So we read, "We have obtained like precious faith through the righteousness of God and our Saviour Jesus Christ." Precious faith, precious faith. That is the way we get the divine nature; that is the way we get the promises of God. That is the way we get all things that pertain to life and godliness. That is God's secret that opens all the treasures of power. That is God's key that unlocks all the doors of grace. That is God's way of access by which His helpless children can come near and receive of His fullness, Faith. But even this very faith, as we learn from the words, is one of the things that is

215

provided for us. We have obtained like precious faith. We have not *attained*, but we have *obtained* it. We have not grown into it, but we have received it as a gift of God's sovereign grace. Obtained; what is obtained? It is something given. How then am I to get the faith that will lift me up into God's life? It is as freely given as the rest. I have heard of people falling over the Alps and getting down into the valleys so low that no rope or cable ever could reach them. We hear their cries, and we have no way of getting down to them. They have not arms long enough to reach up, and those above have not arms long enough to reach down, and they are left there with no way of getting out. I have seen lots of people that way. I think there are plenty of people here this morning that way. I know there is power; I know there are all things that I need. I know that Christ has grace and riches for me. I know that it is my fault, but I cannot get hold of it, I cannot reach them. Blessed be God, as we sometimes sing, "IT REACHES ME." It reacheth me; you cannot reach up to it, but it comes down to your level, and not only does it let down a cable and a rope, but it lets down the arms that take hold of the rope, too. For He says we have obtained precious faith as well as precious promises. Oh, it is great, is it not, and good, to give us these promises? These forty thousand ropes that are hanging down from the throne, each of them a great and precious promise as long as the way to Heaven, and as strong as the throne. Here they are hanging from God's word, just like great cords of love and strength, every one of them seemingly for you. But how am I to get hold of them, you say. Oh, they reach up so high, I cannot get at them. Praise be to God!

There is the precious faith that takes the precious promise. The precious promise drops down from Heaven, and the precious faith reaches up from our helplessness to it. Thus we have obtained the precious faith, as well have gained the precious promise. Oh, how

216

many heartaches would many of us have been saved, how many desperate discouragements, how many years of floundering, if we had learned a little sooner that He that gives us the promise gives us also the faith to take that promise. That is just where half of God's people are sticking, and stumbling, and falling altogether. They believe that God is able to do it. They believe that He is willing to do it. They believe that these promises are for it, but they say, I cannot grasp them! It is because they are trying to grasp them in their own nature, trying to grasp them with their own faith, and not letting God come into them in their absolute helplessness and nothingness, and breathe into them the faith as well as the salvation, the power to take, as well as the thing He gives. Beloved, have you learned these lessons? Have you found your faith fail you? I have. I expect you have; but oh, when it has failed me, I thank God He showed me there was in Christ a willingness and a provision to come into this doubting heart, and just put his trust there, and now when any great and precious promise meets me, and I cannot claim it, I say, "Lord, I am glad I cannot, for then I would try in my own strength to do it. Lord Jesus Christ, grant me the power to claim it, and embrace it, and receive it and hold it. And then I find Him breathing into my heart such an illumination, such a confidence, such a blessed facility in trusting Him, and I have His faith, praise the Lord. Then the next temptation is to attempt to keep it, but I find I cannot keep it. You are no more able to keep faith than to make it, and just remember He says: I am as ready every moment of your life to renew your faith, maintain your faith, support your faith, and be your faith, and you just willing and helpless to let Me be all and all, carried by Me, and yet co-operating with me.

And now, beloved, understand this simple lesson. First, God has called you to glory and to virtue. Secondly, that He has provided all the resources.

Thirdly, that Christ has bought this as a right by His blood and obedience. Fourthly, that He has given a title to it in forty thousand promises. Fifthly, that not only does He give you the promises, but God Himself in His very nature will be the power to keep them and the life of your holiness. Sixthly, that the very faith to grasp and hold them is obtained, through the righteousness of Christ, as part of the purchase of His blood for you and me.

Now just a word as we close about the way in which we are to follow this up. Having entered thus upon the Christian life, and given all indulgence add to your faith. You have got the faith. Now, this faith is a kind of a magnet, to which you can add anything you need. Just as you have seen a magnet pick up a little bit of iron, and then have a dozen bits clinging to it, and so this precious faith just picks up and adds to itself all the things you need in your Christian life. Now then, having got this principle of faith like a mighty magnet in your heart, add to your faith all the graces of the Christian life. Add to your faith virtue, which means courage; it is the old word "vir" – man. Add to your faith courage; be strong and brave, but how? Work it up yourself? Oh, yes, I am going to be strong and brave! Well, try, and then let the devil try, and see how you are tomorrow morning. You cannot make divine courage. Add it to your faith! How is that? Take it from Christ, from His heart, take Christ's courage. By faith draw it out of Him. You cannot draw it out of the depths of your own heart. You may draw up from that well all you like, and you will still find the muddy waters of cowardice, but add to your faith Christ's courage. He never failed; He never feared. He sets His face like a flint, and He said, "I know I shall not be ashamed."

If Christ is in you, you will do just the same. When you find the need of courage, do not try to be courageous, but draw it out of Christ's heart. Add to

218

your faith, that is, just reach out a hand and take it from Him. Faith is just a gift to man, and God the giver, and you take and He gives, and you are then a partaker of the divine nature; you are just taking the divine nature; that is all it is. You are just a helpless, weak human nothing, with a hand that draws out of Christ all your strength. How is it in nature? Let a cloud that is negative in its electric force, approach a cloud that is positive, and you will find that it draws the electricity out of that cloud to its need; and so let a weak human heart reach out in its weakness to Christ, and it draws its strength from Him and adds to its need His own fulness and strength.

Then go on and add to your faith, knowledge, temperance, patience, godliness, brotherly kindness, charity. These qualities must also come from Christ. Knowledge is a wider, more intelligent understanding of Christ's fulness and the reception of Him according as your knowledge grows. Temperance is the divine power of self-restraint, self-denial, self-government. Patience is the spirit of gentleness, endurance and forbearance, sweetness in trial, whether from circumstances of God's providence, or from other people. This must come from God, too. Godliness is the grave and devout spirit in which we just walk under the shadow of the Almighty, and our life seems to carry with it a sense of the divine presence; the idea of singleness of purpose to God, consecration, and a life that is godly. Brotherly kindness, is the spirit of genial love to the brethren of God's household. Such people you love to meet carrying a warm balmy air about them; mellow Christians, not stiff and crusty and unapproachable, but full of the sweetness, the tenderness, and the heavenly affinities of Christ's life. Charity is love in its wider sense, to all men whether Christians or not. Love is a perfect bond, encircling all, whether God's people or not. It is not the love of two, or eight, or ten, or your family or your church, but a love like Christ's, loving in the divine nature, and loving all.

Now, then, He tells you that if you have these things and live this life you will not be barren nor unfruitful, but you will be the fruitful Christian, and wherever you go there will spring up on every side the plants of righteousness, and the fruits of grace. Moreover, He tells you if you do not have these things you will soon lose what you have got. If you do not grow in Christian life, you will forget before long that you were purged from your old sins, and you will hardly know whether you are saved or not. Do we not meet Christians all the time that do not know they are Christians. Why is this? Because they did not go on; they stopped at the beginning, and then lost the very consciousness; perhaps not the fact, but they have lost the assurance of what they had. They have forgotten that they were purged from their old sins; they are blind and cannot see afar off.

But if you *go on* in this way, you will never stumble. The word fall, means stumble. How is it so many stumble? Because they have not gone on in a life of Christ, and entered into his fulness. They are poor emaciated babies, trying to walk before they are sufficiently fed and matured, and so they tumble, and some of them pierce themselves through with many sorrows. The way to keep steadfast is to go on. It is the only way I know.

Again he says, if you will go on in this Christian life, starting thus and growing thus, you shall find abundant entrance into the everlasting kingdom of our Lord and Saviour Jesus Christ. For he is coming soon, and there will be two kinds of Christians. There will be the foolish virgins rushing with wild outcries for the oil and the robes, and finding the door shut, amid shame and despair; and there will be those who were ready, robed and waiting, and that enter in with an abundant and glorious procession. One, like the ship coming home, all
220

battered and half-wrecked, its flag dishonored, and its crew sick and quarantined away off yonder on that island, because the pestilence is on board. I think there are Christians who are going up to the Gates of Heaven and will have to be quarantined a while. I do not know how, but I would not like to see them come into Heaven, in the state of mind that they lay on the death-bed. There are pastors who can easily call up before their minds, people that they have prayed for, who have come at last to the dark hour, and the hurry and rush and the fright, and amidst all, the anxious cry, "Pray for me," the moment's delirium, and then the returning reason, and the shadow of the strange agony, and the moan and the cry, "Oh, if God would only give me back a little while of life; I would not like to die thus. I am not ready; my work is not done. God showed me things to do, and I have not done them. God showed me promises of His grace, and I have not received them. Oh, that I could live a little while." Oh, beloved, I have prayed for weeks and weeks for such men and women, and had my heart ache with living agony and sorrow, as I took hold of Heaven, fasting and praying, sometimes days and nights, that God would give them back their life, but it was too late. I hardly know how they went through. They lay there on that death-bed just like the ship in quarantine, and at last in a stupor they passed away, saved perhaps, but as by fire. But I have seen them also, like the ship coming home from the battle, with its banners streaming, and its crew and captain bearing the scars of battle, but their faces shining with triumph, and welcomed back again by the thousands and tens of thousands.

I passed through Paris after the siege. I never saw a meaner sight on earth. I had heard of the proud French capital, and I looked up at its palaces, and they were full of horses, and its gardens full of straw and manure. Its beautiful buildings were spotted like a face covered with the small-pox. I saw not a wall but was battered with

221

shot and shell. Its lovely cemetery was a deep embankment, and every little while I saw the marks of blood, as I thus passed through the proud city of gaiety. Just a few weeks before, I had gone through Germany. I had seen the battalions of Germany entering through the archways in triumph under mountains of flowers, amid thousands of triumphant voices, as they shouted and cheered and sang the songs of the Fatherland. I saw the marks of fatigue and suffering, and I saw the faded uniforms, but Oh, there was a glow on those faces. They were triumphant with the glory of the victory, and they had an abundant entrance into their old home. And that is the way it is going to be by and by. There are two ways of going in. The Lord is coming, beloved, and then there will be a difference. You can have an easy time if you want it now, but I never found the easy way easy yet – never, and never will. There is the other way of marching up the heavenly street, to ground your arms at Jesus' feet, while you hear the heavenly chorus of those that have gained the victory and the song, "Unto Him be the glory, forevermore."

It is coming fast. The Lord is at hand. He has got work for us, that will crowd us every minute until he comes. He has given us all things that pertain to life and godliness. He has given us His own nature. Oh, this morning, I want to take it all. Oh, this morning, I want to meet Him. Oh beloved, let us reach out our hands and grasp those ropes of promise, those exceeding great and precious promises, that divine heart. That is all we need for our insufficiency, and an abundant entrance into the everlasting kingdom of our Lord and Saviour Jesus Christ

NICOSIA.

CHAPTER XIX.

CHRISTIAN LIFE IN
THE EPISTLES OF JOHN.

For the life was manifested, and we have seen it, and bear witness, and show unto you that eternal life, which was with the Father and was manifested unto us. – 1Jn. 1:2.

*H*OW MUCH of personal interest attaches to the letters of our friends. If you send a book to a friend, perhaps it will not be read, even if printed on handsome paper, in attractive type, and beautifully bound. But sit down and write a letter to that friend, and how eagerly it will be read. Not a word will be overlooked, for it is filled with personal interest, tenderness that no book can possess. If you write it yourself, it will be sure to be read. Letters are expressions of confidence and friendship. They are channels of the deepest human affection. Some of the best books ever written have been letters.

So the Holy Ghost, when He would speak some tender thought, or bring back some sweet memory, did not say to His servants, "Write a book." He knew better. The Holy Ghost wrote letters. The whole of the New Testament is a bundle of letters. When God wished to say something to His people He sat down and wrote them a letter. The word *epistles* sounds like heavy artillery, but when I call them letters to a friend, and believe in reading them, they are letters God has written to me, I shall find indeed the light of Heaven is shining through them.

We have before us this morning the sweetest and fullest of all these New Testament letters, and I trust we

225

shall know as never before, of having this first epistle of John written on our heart and life, that truly our fellowship may be with the Father and with His Son Jesus Christ. So will the promise of the next verse be fulfilled in us. These things write we unto you, that your joy may be full.

I.

The first thing that strikes us in this epistle is THE BLOOD. The first thought perhaps in the letter is Jesus and the last is the same. But the first thing John looks at in Him is the blood. "The blood of Jesus Christ His Son cleanseth us from all sin." All blessing comes through it. It not only cleanses, but it is carried up into Heaven and intercedes for us there. It is a complete covering for our sin. Even St. John could never get away from the cross, but lived constantly under its droppings. This is the resting-place of all pure lives, under the constant cleansing of the Lord Jesus Christ.

The blood not only cleanses us at conversion. It does a great deal more. In yonder Heaven it pleads for us. It is a daily cleansing from frailties. It is not only justification, in is cleansing in a larger sense. It is a living fountain, the blood of a living Christ. It comes into us and cleanses us from all sin, and keeps us pure and sweet. It pardons, and it keeps us accepted; but it does more. It is the life of our being. Moses understood this very well. In the old tabernacle service the blood was not only poured out, but a part was kept and carried into the Holy of Holies and left there. So the blood of Christ was shed for us, but the blood is also imparted to us. Not the blood only, but the living principle of the blood. The blood shed for us atones for our sin, but beloved, can you grasp this other thought. It is life forevermore. That is the meaning of the blood of Jesus Christ in us. Christ's life is in us, a part of our own conscience life, thus giving us His own nature. Blood is sometimes said to be thicker than water. That means relationship. If Christ's blood is in us, it does make us partakers of His divine nature. It goes through all our frames, giving new vigor and life, and sustaining us by the very life of Christ. Physicians have sometimes saved the lives of their patients by infusing into their veins some of their own life blood. So Christ's blood in us makes us constantly victorious, and keeps us always pure.

"Through all my soul its currents flow,
Through all my nature stealing;
And deep within my soul I know,
The consciousness of healing."

II.

THE SPIRIT is next spoken of in this letter, after the blood. It is the next great landmark or mountain peak in the landscape. "Ye have an unction from the Holy One." – 1Jn. 2:20. "The anointing which ye have received of Him abideth in you" (2:27). That is the abiding Holy Ghost. The oil is the symbol of the divine Paraclete, who is shed forth as a light, a healer, a teacher. He brings Christ to us as the atmosphere brings the sun. The sun is ninety millions of miles away, but it is in this house this morning. So Jesus is in Heaven, but He is here too. How? The Holy Spirit brings Him. His life is shed forth by the Holy Ghost. There is nothing in this passage to discountenance any teaching that brings Christ's life to the hearer, any more than it is necessary for us to do without gas or windows, because they are not sunlight. It is nonsense to say we have no need of them. The servants of Christ's, His ministers and evangelists are just little windows letting in the light of God, and that is the meaning of this passage, "Ye need not that any man teach you." God is speaking through that man. We do not need man to teach us as man, but our ears should ever be open to the Holy Ghost, no matter through whom He speaks.

Beloved, have we got this anointing. Do we know what it is when the voice of teachers falls upon your ear to say, "It is the Lord!" It is sweet to sit and listen to some servant of God giving a thought which has been whispered to your own heart before and wonder, "Where did you get that?" It was the Lord who had been speaking to both. Dear ones, do you know that voice? It comes sometimes as a warning cry, "That is not God's word," and though an angel of Heaven speak the word, you cannot listen to it or receive it.

Have we got this anointing in our hearts, beloved? Is He speaking in the secret of our soul! Is the word broken up there for you? As mothers break up food for their babes, so God wants to prepare His bread for us, and enable us to minister it to others.

III.

SONSHIP is the next theme in this epistle. The blood links us with the Son and the anointing with the Holy Ghost. Now the next great word lifts us to the Father.

"Behold, what manner of love the Father hath bestowed upon us, that we should be called the sons of God!" He hath bestowed not adoption but sonship. "Called" sons might mean adoption, but in the second verse the word in the Greek expresses, as no other word can, that we ARE the sons of God.

Then, too, "the manner" of it is so precious. It is sweetly, grandly, graciously bestowed. He treats us with kingly, lofty courtesy. He shows us He counts us princes of Heaven, members of the aristocracy there. There is no condescension in this, but the equality of love. We may come to Him and bow to kiss His feet, but He lifts us up

228

and places us by His side. "Behold what manner of love." We are now even as the Son.

IV.

ABIDING, next follows. The other word for this is Fellowship. Have you thus entered into union with Him? If so you must keep it, or rather let Him keep it for you. He will keep you in constant communion with Himself if you will let Him. This is the anointing that abideth. It will not let you go. This anointing keeps from sin. In chap. 5:18, it is spoken of as keeping us so close that the Evil One toucheth us not, because the inner life is so shut round by the presence of the Son. A more perfect translation brings this meaning out more clearly. Jesus is the only-begotten, and "He keepeth him, so that Wicked One toucheth him not." There is room here to get closer, closer, closer. Let it be so close in these hallowed days, that we shall feel His presence and no cloud shall be between, or fear or rebuke, for He has promised, "I will not be wroth with thee nor rebuke thee." Then that wicked one shall not be able to touch us. We may hear his voice warring outside, but the tabernacle within his filthy feet shall never be able to defile so long as we are abiding under the shadow of the Almighty.

V.

SINLESSNESS, purity of life and walk is next spoken of. He that abideth sinneth not. If you have any controversy about this, you must settle it with John. Have you never seen from some old rotten log a sprout growing, fresh and pure, a new tree starting up from the midst of earthworms and decay that you would not touch, yet the new growth was perfectly clean and pure? That is what God means about us, beloved. All around us is of earth, but in the midst is new life that is as incapable of sin as

229

God Himself. To say that the divine life within us sins is to say that God sins. We may step back into the old life, but the seed that God gives cannot sin, for it is born from above. A passenger on the ocean may be surrounded by wild waves, full of dirt and mire, but the porthole is closed and they can't get in. But let the porthole be left open even for a little, and the bucket full that will enter will give more trouble than all the whole ocean outside. It did not get in because the ship was unseaworthy or the captain incompetent, but because of your neglect. So in our lives sinlessness is linked with abiding in Him, and failure springs from needless, negligent, and wicked departure from your place of fellowship with Jesus.

VI.

LOVE comes next. It runs from the eleventh verse of the third chapter on through the fourth. Without this love which is the sum and substance, the very essence of this whole epistle, all the rest goes for nothing. May the Lord open to us this wonderful chapter of love like a beautiful garden of blossoms so that we shall want to stay in its sweetness and fragrance all our life.

1. This love is God's very essence and nature.

2. Without this love we cannot understand or know God.

3. This love springs from confidence and faith, "because He first loved us."

4. This love comes from the presence of Christ in us. "Herein is our love made perfect, that we may have boldness in the day of judgment: because as He is, so are we in this world." That is, the way to have our love made perfect, is not to love in our own strength, but let Christ love in us. Then it cannot be kept back.

There are two unpardonable sins in the Word, one against Jesus, the other against love. He that rejecteth Him, perisheth, but he that loves not perishes not. These

230

two sins will debar from yonder Heaven alike. God is love, and we haven't got the victory of God if we haven't the victory of love. May we from our hearts be able to say, "Herein is our love made perfect." Not the old natural love but the new. "As I have loved you." I have many times been asked the question, "Why cannot I overcome right here in this matter of love," and I have often felt like saying, "Are you quite sure you *want* to overcome there? Are you sure you want to love there?" and more than once I have been told, "I never saw that before; I don't believe I do want to love there. It has been a real satisfaction to hate instead." That is not being made perfect in love. Oh, how blessed, wherever you go to be able to rain down showers of love. It is sweeter for you, my brother, than for the one you love. I am far more afraid of the sting of hate and its bitterness in my own soul than in the one I dislike.

VII.

CONFIDENCE AND VICTORY is the theme of the fifth chapter. It is pointed out all through by the words "We know." This blessed knowledge is a real experience. It is not conviction or ideas, or thinking, but knowing. A real touch of something divine. Before that knowledge all sophistries vanish away.

Three forms of assurance are mentioned:

1. We know we have eternal life. This is founded simply on the record, the promise of His Word. Not to believe it is to make Him a liar. And if we believe it we know we have what it promises. This is the simple secret of assurance: to come to Christ and claim His promise, and then absolutely believe we have what He has promised. This assurance of faith must precede, in the logical and divine order all other kinds of assurance and witness and all interior consciousness. He that believeth hath the witness in himself.

231

2. We know we have the petitions that we asked of Him. Careful to ask only what is in accordance with His will and Word, the same simple faith in that Word again brings the same assurance, "We know we have." This is God's prerequisite condition of answered prayer. And it is just as simple as the assurance of salvation already referred to. If we know that what we asked is within His Word and thus His will, we know it is ours, and we rest and praise.

3. We know that He hath given us an understanding that we are in Him that is true even in His Son Jesus Christ. This is the assurance and consciousness of our deeper union with the person of Jesus. This is what He promised through the coming of the Holy Ghost, "At that day ye shall know that I am in the Father and ye in Me and I in you."

And this confidence gives us the victory over the world and over that wicked one that toucheth us not. Blessed assurance! Blessed victory! Blessed Jesus!

VIII.

The last thought of all is Christ Himself, the overshadowing thought of the epistle. The secret of all real joy and peace is the living person of Jesus. Two brothers met in a distant land, each speaking a different language, yet both children of God, and unable to understand the other. But they had both learned one word, and they pointed to it and said "Jesus." Then they gazed into each other's face and clasped hands and said it over and over again, Jesus! Jesus! Jesus! Theirs was the sweetest fellowship in all that hotel. Others were chattering around them; they knew only one word, but it was more than all the rest.

So the thoughts and themes we have been speaking of are but mountain peaks. The great substratum of eternal rock is Jesus Himself, and the sublime summary of the
232

whole epistle is this: "We know that the Son of God hath come and hath given us an understanding to know Him that is true, and we are in. Him that is true and in His Son Jesus Christ. This IS THE TRUE GOD AND ETERNAL LIFE." Yes He is the substance of the cleansing and the anointing and the sonship and the fellowship and the love and the confidence and the victory. So leaning with John upon His breast, let us learn to know Himself more tenderly and intimately.

> "More dear, more intimately nigh
> Than even the closest earthly tie.
> Nearer, dearer, still to me,
> Thou living, loving, Saviour be,
> Brighter the vision of Thy face;
> More charming still Thy words of grace.
> So life shall be transformed to love;
> A Heaven below, a Heaven above."

CHAPTER XX.

CHRISTIAN LIFE IN THE EPISTLE OF JUDE

"But ye, beloved, building up yourselves on your most holy faith, praying in the Holy Ghost. Keep yourselves in the love of God, looking for the mercy of our Lord Jesus Christ unto eternal life. And of some have compassion, making a difference: And others save with fear, pulling them out of the fire; hating even the garment spotted by the flesh. Now unto him that is able to keep you from falling, and to present you faultless before the presence of his glory with exceeding joy, To the only wise God our Saviour, be glory and majesty, dominion and power, both now and forever. Amen." – Jude 20-25.

THE BOOK OF JUDE is a picture of the declension and apostasy of many in the primitive church of God, one of the signs of the coming of the Son of Man. Even in the days of Jude it was necessary to contend earnestly for the faith once delivered to the saints. "For there are certain men crept in unawares, who were before of old ordained to this condemnation, ungodly men, turning the grace of our God into lasciviousness, and denying the only Lord God, and our Lord Jesus Christ." – Jude 4.

The letter is a series of warnings to the church about the danger of these departures, and the principles upon which they are dealt with by God. Three examples are given of God's judgment on them who turned away from Him:

I. The children of Israel, ver. 5.

II. The fallen angels, ver. 6.

III. Sodom and Gomorrah, ver. 7.

Three pictures are given is this epistle:
I. The picture of a worldly church.
II. The picture of true Christians.
III. The picture of the Lord Himself.

I.

The worldly church. In verse eleven three types sum up the three forms of declension from God, viz.: the way of Cain, the error of Balaam, the gainsaying of Core, or Korah.

1. The way of Cain was the way of unbelief in the blood of Christ. He rejected it and depended on his own works, his own righteousness and morality. His offering expressed no faith in the blood of the Lamb. He despised God's way of atonement for sin. The cross of Jesus divides the world today into two classes. One denies the blood and brings flowers and fruits instead, but this soon leads to the stain of murder and every other sin. Reject the blood and soon will come envy, hate, jealousy, and worldliness. Cain went away to the land of Nod east of Eden, and there was soon surrounded with culture and art. This followed rejecting the blood and love and will of God. Musical instruments, and working in brass and iron all come in the way of Cain. The first beginning of apostasy is getting away from the blood of the Lamb. It is the way of Cain. If you do not like the blood you will get blood on you before you are through.

2. The error of Balaam. This is a type of a different sin from the other. This man wished to obey God on the one hand and please Balak on the other. He loved the wages of unrighteousness. He was a compromising man, the precursor of a long list in the Bible of which Demas brings up the rear in the New Testament. He had no real hold on God, and before long found a way to get the wages of unrighteousness and defile the children of

236

Israel, in the midst of which he fell himself under the sword of vengeance. There was a wider and wider divergence in his course from the right path till, like one of the pilgrims who started for the city of Zion, before long he found that city behind him and himself, facing again the city of destruction. Love not the world is the lesson this teaches. The language here is exceedingly strong. They ran greedily after the error of Balaam. They were avaricious, going after their unlimited, unrestrained desire. Their chief aim was their own pleasure. Sin has an accelerated movement, until the running ends in the final plunge into the pit of Korah. Sin does not go rapidly always. It begins gently and imperceptibly but it slides gradually into a quicker motion and finally ends in a plunge into the bottomless abyss.

3. The gainsaying of Korah. This prince of Israel became tired of the rule of Moses and the priesthood of Aaron. He was not willing to submit to them, and rose in proud disobedience and rebellion against them and so against God, for it is written "He that despiseth you despiseth Me." He that rejected Moses and Aaron, God's servants and appointed ministers and teachers rejected God. These men rose in presumption, rebellion and disobedience against the authority of God's church and people. The next step was soon taken, open defiance. "Humble yourselves therefore under the mighty hand of God." "Be clothed with humility." " Pride goeth before destruction." This same spirit of Korah is in the world today, the spirit of independence and license, demanding freedom and throwing off all authority in the home and the state. Socialists, Nihilists, the bomb throwers of Chicago, are all precursors of the lawlessness of anti-Christ.

The three forms of evil we are especially guarded against in this epistle are the unbelief of Cain, the spirit of Balaam, who began where Cain ended in worldliness,

237

and finally the disobedience of Korah. One act of disobedience may soon lead to open rebellion and defiance of God. There is no license given in God's word to the most trifling act of disobedience. It is the essence of sin to dare to admit the right to disobey in the smallest trifle. It is the spirit of Korah and may end in apostasy and rebellion. It is written in fiery letters all over the history of the past, that the disobedient shall perish. That is a terrible figure, given in the Old Testament of the old prophet of God who was sent to cry out against Jeroboam's sin, and who so fearlessly obeyed. When the king stretched out his arm against him; at the word of faith that arm shriveled up, and at the word of prayer it was restored again. But before the next day closed the dead body of the old prophet was lying by the wayside. He was slain by the indignation of God, because he had dared to disobey Him. An old prophet like himself had seduced him, pretending to have a revelation, and he perished, because he dared to listen to him after God had spoken to him. In all this there are three steps, first, going easily, then a faster descent and then the plunge. It is like getting in the Maelstrom off Norway. The motion is imperceptible at first, then it gently increases, gets faster and faster; now the boat is whirling in a circle, and now madly rushing into the awful vortex. So in human life bitter strife and jealousies and envy draw the heart further and further from God. At first it seems but little, but ere long the heart is running greedily in the error of Balaam, and the end is the plunge of the cataract.

II.

Let us look now at the other picture given in the twentieth verse:

"But ye, beloved, building up yourselves on your most holy faith, praying in the Holy Ghost, keep yourselves in the love of God."

238

1. The element in Christian character that is opposed to the unbelief of Cain is faith, the most important of all the graces.

2. It is most holy faith. It leads to purity of heart, of life, of word, and of deed. It is not possible to keep faith without obedience. "Holding a good conscience, which some having put away concerning faith have made shipwreck." If the conscience is not kept clear, pure, and open before God, it is not possible to believe. Most holy faith is faith that leads to obedience.

3. This faith is to be built up. It is to be constantly growing, maturing. Faith begins as a holy thing, but it grows after that. It is complete faith at first, but it is like the completion of a baby. It is all there, all the parts, but it has to grow up into manhood. Christ gives a clean heart, or better, He gives His heart, but it is an infant life. It is infant holiness. Afterward there must be growth. We are to build on day by day, expecting more of Christ in us, and getting more, and so growing up in Him. Today there is more of His life in us than yesterday; tomorrow more than today. The next day there is a still higher mount to climb. There will come more victories with more life.

4. How is this growth to be obtained? By praying in the Holy Ghost and keeping in the love of God. We will not have much of the divine element of holy faith in us unless we feed it day by day with prayer. We must live a life of constant prayer. Praying in the Holy Ghost means simply this: When the Holy Ghost comes He comes as a loving person and takes charge of the whole life, planning for us, watching over us, fitting into our every need for every moment, there is not a moment but He is trying to pray in you some prayer. Watch the Holy Ghost and vigilantly obey His least whisper. He takes charge of the spiritual development and will not let anything be lost, but fills up in life all the fulness of God's highest will.

The element in this growth is love. We must have the spirit of confidence or we shall not grow. We need to hear His whisper every moment, "My darling child!" We must know that He is not wroth with us. If there is any cloud of condemnation over us we will not grow. We must have God ever with us to grow. The least shadow of sin or judgment will hinder our growth. We must sweetly rest in God's bosom always, and so keep ourselves in His love, being ever obedient to His will.

5. What is the outlook of this life? We are to build up on our most holy faith here by prayer and love, but we are to look for something better. There is an upper chamber from whose windows we can see the land that is very far off. This is to be a life of confidence and its pole-star the hope of His coming.

1. Beloved, have you entered into this life of faith? Has it given you justification and holiness forever?

2. Are you growing in this life?

3. Is it a life of prayer in the Holy Ghost?

4. Is it a life of love? Are you keeping in the love of God? Is it the land of Beulah with sweet perfumes upon the breeze?

5. What is your attitude to the future? Are you turning with bright face toward the sun rising or the sun setting? Are you looking for His coming?

III.

Jude gives one more picture in his epistle, that of the Lord Himself, ver. 24-25.

God is able to keep us from falling. He has just been speaking about the people who stumble in the intervening verses. There is a difference between falling away and falling by the way. If a person falls away, he is an apostate, and there is no hope for him. If you should stumble, get up quickly and go on again, even if the face is all scarred and the garments torn. But there is no need of stumbling. I don't think that all of you honestly believe God is able to keep you from stumbling. You say it is not possible for you or any man to keep from falling. Of course not. But God is able to keep you. Has He not all dominion. The doxology at the close of this letter so declares. Has He not dominion over you as well as over nature? Do you give God the right to have dominion over you? You know He is able and He would pour in on your soul such a glory as never has been there, if you would see that it is possible never to lose the sweetness of His smile, never to be down in the dust again. It is a solemn trust to carry the standard of the Lord, and it will be a proud moment when you hand it back to Him, never having been taken by the enemy. We are under a power that is able to keep us above every loss, every temptation that can possibly come to us. If we have in our heart the thought that we have got to fall, let us take it out as unfit to be there. It will make the heart weaker to resist Satan. He is able to keep you from slipping. Not perhaps from what the world may think a slip. The world does not know as God sees in your heart. There may be errors of judgment, but what the world calls an error of judgment may be for you an act of obedience to God. They that please all men cannot please God. It is enough to carry in the breast at all times the sweet consciousness of pleasing Him.

Then there is another thought. He is not only able to keep us here, but He is able to present us faultless there. If we let Him do it, it will be with exceeding joy. This is not being barely saved. They that keep their garments here undefiled shall shine in the kingdom of the Father, and sit with Christ upon His throne. Let that thought be with us evermore. We can be *without blame* here, kept from all willful disobedience. But there shall be without fault in the presence of His glory. We do not know how this is to be done. The power belongs to God. I lay myself in the dust, for I cannot do it. I lay you in the dust for you cannot do it. Failure is stamped on all our endeavors, worthless are all our efforts. But He is able to keep you from stumbling, able to save to the uttermost, able to present you faultless. Unto Him be the glory forever and ever. Amen.

CHAPTER XXI

CHRISTIAN LIFE IN
THE PERSONAL EPISTLES; OR,
THE COURTESIES OF CHRISTIAN LIFE.

---

*T*HE three epistles to Philemon, Kurida, the elect Lady, and the well beloved Gaius, may be called the personal epistles. They teach us some very precious lessons.

Personal correspondence is a very useful way of witnessing for Christ. The friendly letter is often the best evidence of personal character and the most effectual channel of influence. Are our letters to these we love given to the Holy Spirit and really consecrated channels of service.

I. – PHILEMON.

This epistle is the highest example of Christian tact to be found in the Bible.

Back of it was the story of a runaway slave named Onesimus, who had left his master Philemon at Colosse and turned up at Rome. His name Onesimus "profitable," had been strangely contradicted by his life. He had stolen money from his master and given him little cause to remember him as a source of either profit or pleasure. But in the drift of the great city, he was thrown into the company of Paul and the power of Christ's love and grace in that great heart soon won the recreant slave for Christ. There Paul found that he was the property of his old friend Philemon. The question of duty was soon decided. He must return to his master and make matters right and then Philemon himself must direct the rest. Paul would gladly keep him as a helper in the work, but he will not even think of this without Philemon's own

243

choice. And so he sends him back with this letter to his master, and out of this little episode we have the finest example of Christian delicacy and courtesy in the annals of religious life. After the first loving salutation to himself and family, he approaches the delicate master of Onesimus by a gentle reference to his apostolic right and authority and then withdraws it and rests his plea on the tenderer ground of love, adding with a touch of deep pathos a hint of his old age and his great sufferings for Jesus Christ. With a bold stroke of his pen he then at once introduces Onesimus as his own son, whom he has begotten in the Lord, and softens at once the severity of the shock which this must bring to Philemon at first by a witty play upon the word Onesimus, a little dash of humor provoking a smile and giving time to the reader to recover from the shock of the previous sentence. Then he proceeds to tell in fuller detail why he was thus sent him, not because he had wanted to get rid of him, for he would have highly valued him as a helper in the Gospel, and still should, if Philemon chooses to grant him with his own mind but from the most delicate regard to Philemon's rights and with the thought that perhaps he was to be Philemon himself a greater boon than to Paul as he now received him not as a slave but as a brother for ever.

Then follows that majestic stroke of Gospel liberty which struck the death blow to ancient and modern slavery.

"Not now as a slave but as a brother beloved, specially to me, but how much more to thee both in the flesh and in the Lord. If thou count me therefore a partner receive him as myself." That was a telling blow at human slavery. That was the greatest plea for human equality ever made. We can only understand it fully when we realize what ancient slavery was. The Roman bond slave was the absolute property of his master. On one occasion four hundred Roman slaves were ordered to be executed because one of them, unknown had committed a crime and the guilty one could not be detected. With no hope in their life they had nothing to hold them back from the most terrible vices. To suggest to a master to receive a slave as a brother, nay even as Paul himself was a bridging over a gulf which even in our most exclusive ideas of caste today we can hardly understand. But this the gospel did. It made the bondman free in God and the Church of God, without interfering with civil questions or touching the delicate matter of Roman law and constitution. It did not attempt with iron hand to break the fetters, but it put such a fire under them as soon melted them away.

This is the true way to remove difficulties. The wind and sun once laid a wager who could first take the coat off a pilgrim. The wind began. It blew and stormed and made his garments shake and tremble in its violence, and again and again it had almost blown the old coat away. But the shivering pilgrim drew it the more tightly round him and held on his way with a firmer hold upon its covering folds. Then the sun began. There was not one wild blast of fury or seeming power, but his gentle warmth fell upon the traveler, with cheering radiance and then with hotter breath, until the old pilgrim began to unfasten his garment, and ere noon had thrown it across his arm and was walking up the hill with the sweat streaming down his face, in his lightest possible garb, while the sun seemed laughing in every ray at his easy victory.

So the Gospel of Jesus Christ melts away the troubles, which violence, rashness, resolution, socialism and human policy try in vain to correct. It has been truly said, that while bleeding at every pore Christianity has gone forth to staunch all the wounds of humanity, while herself bound and imprisoned like the aged Paul, she has gone through the ages to open the prison doors and set the captives free, and while ever more giving up her own life unto the death, she has brought life and hope eternal to dying perishing men.

But in all this beneficence there is an exact sense of justice. First the noble apostle had already said "Whom I would have retained but without thy mind would I do nothing." And now here he adds, "If he hath wronged thee, or oweth thee aught put that on mine account. I Paul have written it with mine own hand, (a regular promissory note) I will repay it." The highest generosity must ever recognize the principles of justice and the rights of every human being; and the truest Christian will ever be most sensitive to the rights of others, and the strictest integrity and honesty in all the questions of business and money.

Then he closes his exquisite letter with four personal touches of rare grace and power. First he reminds Philemon of how much more he owes to him as his spiritual father than all the favors he could claim.

Next he appeals for this act of courtesy and generosity as a personal favor, comfort and refreshing him in his lone prison.

Next with fine tact he stops all his pleading and almost apologizes for having said so much, assuring his friend of his generous confidence that he will do all this and more than he asks.

And, finally, he crowns it all by intimating that he is himself coming soon to visit him, and asking him to prepare him a lodging, not saying in so many words, but letting us read between the lines, and it is scarcely likely that Philemon failed to read it too, that he would expect to find things all right when he arrived.

Surely we have had a divine example of the true way to rule human hearts, the glorious equality in Christ of all God's children, the regard we owe to the rights and feelings of others, the forgiveness of injuries, the restitution of wrongs, the value of tact and gentleness, good humour, and even consecrated wit in the service of

Christ, and the infinite delicacy and-fitness of the grace of Christ for the adjustment of every difficulty in life and the right discharge of every duty and trust.

II. – SECOND JOHN.

This letter was written to a Christian matron named Kuria, residing probably at Ephesus, and perhaps one of the friends and hostesses of the Church of Christ there during the Apostle's ministry. After giving us a fine example of the purity and simplicity of Christian friendship and fellowship, he adds a few general sentences about the practical side of Christian life as manifested in holy obedience, and warns her and her family against the seductions of evil already in the Church and bids her watch against any failure that might lessen aught of her full service and reward. He then comes to what we might call the specific teaching of the Epistle. This is contained in the tenth verse – "If there come any unto you and bring not this doctrine, receive him not into your house, neither bid him God speed for he that biddeth him Good speed is partaker of his evil deeds." Here we have the important fact that we must avoid complicity with or responsibility for false teaching. We cannot work with unscriptural principles or build God's temple with untempered mortar. We cannot judge men's hearts, but we can judge their teachings, and we must stand strictly and only on God's holy word. Whatsoever is not according to this is wrong, and incompatible with our freedom in service, or the permanence of aught we try to do. One hour of work in harmony with God's word, is worth a lifetime of compromise.

III. – THIRD JOHN.

The Third Epistle of John was addressed to Gaius, the name of several esteemed and honored saints in the New Testament.

Two special distinctive lessons come to us from his life. The first is the converse of the last lesson in the Second Epistle, viz the duty and the glory of a true Christian hospitality. What higher commendation can be given to a Christian business man than this. "Beloved thou doest faithfully whatsoever thou doest to the brethren and to strangers, which have borne witness of thy charity before the Church. Whom, if thou bring forward on their journey after a godly sort thou shalt do well. Because for His name's sake they went forth taking nothing of the Gentiles. We therefore ought to receive such that we might be fellow helpers to the truth.

The second special teaching of this letter is the prayer of the Apostle for his friend, for his physical health and temporal prosperity, recognizing both as among God's blessings for his children and connecting both in a very practical and instructive way with His spiritual condition and welfare. Here we touch a great theme and one that is elsewhere more fully discussed. Meanwhile it is very sweet in the last of the letters of the latest of the Apostles to find this inspired prayer pointing surely to the gracious will of our dear Lord for every one of his faithful children. "Beloved, I pray above all things, that thou mayest be in health and prosper even as thy soul prospereth."

CHAPTER XXII.

CHRISTIAN LIFE IN THE APOCALYPSE PART I. – VICTORY

"He that overcometh shall inherit all things; and I will be his God, and he shall be my Son." – Rev. 21:7.

---

*T*HIS text is the keynote of the Christian life unfolded in this apocalypse, namely a life of victory, an overcoming life. It leads us back to the beginning of the book, to the seven pictures given there in the seven letters to the churches in Asia, showing the various aspects of Christian life and also the various aggressive stages of Christianity. They were written to the churches in Asia Minor, clustered around the church of Ephesus where John resided as a sort of patriarch over them all.

The Lord Jesus many years after His ascension came down to Patmos and added a personal letter to these churches, a searching letter, giving each the warning it needed. These letters too, looked out over the ages to come, and the pictures they contained were adapted to the whole Christian church, or to individual Christian need till He shall come again. Each closes with a special promise to him that overcometh. We will look this morning at these seven overcomers who represent every kind of conflict and every kind of trial to be met with in the Christian life. They are seven warriors, fighting the battles of the Lord, and conquering in His name. Each one has a different fight, yet each conflict we have met with or shall meet some day.

249

I.

The first one was written to the church at Ephesus. "To him that overcometh will I give to eat of the tree of life, which is in the midst of the paradise of God."

What is the opposition and enemy over which this victory has been gained? Revelation 2:2, reads, I know thy works. Then follows a long and high inventory of victories already achieved. There has been work, and more work, patience born of trial, resistance to the current wisdom of the day, much labor, pure doctrine, great endurance for Christ's sake. That is a great deal to say of a church. Can it be said of you? Nevertheless the Lord had somewhat against that church. There was outward correctness and much work, but the heart had been neglected. They had not ceased to love, but they had lost the bloom of the first love. They had not guarded the simple sweet fervor of that early fire. They had not lost it; they had left it. They had grown too respectable for it, too dignified for the simplicity of love. They had been encrusted with doctrine and work, but away down in the heart there was the winter of old age and its hoary hairs. The message to them was unless they came back to the simplicity and fervor of those first days, repented and did the first works, they should not only be disapproved but removed out of their place. They should cease to be a church. Unless they came back the Lord would reject them. But if they came back to their early heart religion they should eat of the tree of life.

Dear friends, do we find in our hearts this morning any need of this warning? Have we been guarding the early simplicity of our love to Him? Has He not convicted some of you of this? The Lord is saying to us, I am sure, today, watch the heart, for it is already crumbling and corroding away even in the midst of much work.

This first picture then is of the man who has conquered the spirit of heart declension and holds it by the power of God true to its first love.

II.

He that overcometh shall not be hurt of the second death.

This promise is given to the victor over suffering. Smyrna was the suffering church. The name means myrrh, something bruised. Polycarp, one of the first Christian martyrs, a disciple of John, sealed his love to his Lord with his blood at Smyrna. This church went through a terrible baptism of suffering, a fiery trial of pain and hardship. The second age of Christianity had to endure this to bring it back to its first love, and God gives it always if it is needed to lift the spirit above the world. The promise to those who endure is they shall not be hurt of the second death. They are to bear and become more illustrious in spirit and character. Its object is to separate from man, and man and let the soul learn to stand alone with Jesus Christ. God knows and ever will know the bitterness of it. Never mind the ordeal. You are to be faithful and it shall not hurt you.

Life was promised to the first victor. This has more; the crown of life. It is a kinglier battle than the other. There is more in it than being merely faithful. Trial is sent to win something. From every such conflict some trophy can be gained to the honor and glory of God at the appearing of Jesus Christ. Every gem in the diadem given then may be a tear crystallized into a jewel of glory.

There is not a word of blame given to this suffering church. The Lord is present to sustain and encourage. So in the battle of life it is sufficient to know the Lord loves and supports. His word is "Fear not." Dear ones, are you overcoming the sorrow of your life, or is it overcoming you? Are you lying down under it and fretting, and while not exactly blaming God are you wondering that others have so much easier a lot? Oh you are wrong. There hath no temptation taken you but such as is common. Agony just as deep, testing just as hard, comes to all the children of God every day. In His infinite tenderness He knows all about it, and if we trust Him through it all He will surely give to us the victory and crown of life.

III.

The next message was to the worldly church of Pergamos. Christ goes on to tell the particular perils of this church which had in its membership those who held the doctrine of the Nicolaitans, and also of Balaam, and thus it ran the danger of being seduced by the world. Balaam tried to curse Israel by prophesy and failed, but he succeeded in seducing them through the pleasures of the world. They were drawn off by the attractions of the daughters of Moab and God sent judgment on them.

So the Christians at Pergamos encountered the same thing. In that gay capital they were often invited to Roman entertainments, at which they had to sit down and eat things offered in sacrifice to idols. There was danger of failing to stand with Christ, and of entering into a compromise with the world. Some of them held also the doctrine of the Nicolaitans who believed in justification but not sanctification. They were saved and that was enough. They claimed freedom to do as they pleased. The Lord said, "I hate it." He allows no compromise. His children must be His alone and not at all the world's. To him that overcomes the seductions of the world and its forbidden pleasures, Christ promises to give to eat of the hidden manna, and also to give a white stone, and in the stone a new name written which no man knoweth saving he that receiveth it. That is, He will give His food and friendship. The white stone was a type of intimate and exclusive regard. At these ancient feasts each guest had a marble table given him with his name upon it, and he took it away as a memorial of the entertainment. So, whosoever gives up the world's pleasures and feasts and friendships for Christ, will receive His inner divine life to feed upon, His joys and pleasures, nay, His very heart. The white stone means His friendship. He will call you by a name that no one knows but you and Him. You are taken into His intimate and divine love as a confidential friend, but this cannot be unless the world is first given up. You cannot be feeding on the hidden manna, and enjoying the sweet communion of His precious love unless you are separated unto Him alone. I know there are many here who would not give up the tokens they have received of the Saviour's love and trust for all the smiles and friendships of the world. The Lord will keep proving you. The tests will come in many ways. Satan perhaps will not repeat the enticements of youth; he will attack in some new way, but the Lord will give the victory. It may not come with the blast of a trumpet. It may be quietly given in scenes of deep sorrow and suffering, but with it will come the blessing to the church in Pergamos, the hidden manna and the white stone.

IV.

The message to the church in Thyatira is very strongly marked. The woman Jezebel is in the front of the picture, carrying us back to the days of Ahab and Elijah, the horrible days of Sidonian idolatry. Another expression used is "the depths of Satan." It is a dark picture not of the world but of the wiles of the devil, the allurements of Satan. It is an exact representation of Christianity in the age of corruption, at the time of the rise of Romanism, when that woman in scarlet, the modern Jezebel, for over one thousand years committed

253

adultery with the kings of the earth in a spiritual sense, and led the consciences of men. We are not in such extreme danger of Rome today, but we are in danger of her spirit and her evil master. All the false lights of today, carnal ideas of religious truth, the various forms of spiritualism, are all the wiles of the devil, and the depths of Satan, sent in the last days in counterfeit of the Son of God, and they are most likely to fall into them who in their zeal to avoid error oppose the higher teaching of the gospel. Afraid of being misled, they will not let the Holy Ghost lead them. Conservative men are afraid of the supernatural signs of the times. There is no way of disproving and overcoming the false signs and miracles of the day, but by the true ones. God is working mightily today by the Holy Ghost in healing human bodies. The way to answer the counterfeit is by the reality. We are not to meet the devil by bare denial, but by divine power.

The spirit that is wholly yielded up to God will be filled with the divine life, and will be so anointed with His presence that it shall be kept from error. Beloved there is nothing today that will save us from error but a whole religion. The people who are most in peril of going astray are the people who are most afraid of any new teaching the Spirit may bring. The hard, stern, cold, inflexibly orthodox Christians, not wholly given up to the Holy Ghost, are the very people who are in the most danger of being led into unsound views of truth. That Puritan land of our country, New England, the land that produced Jonathan Edwards, and has stood so firmly for old ideas, but would not receive the Holy Ghost, is today the land of rationalism. Four or five professors in its oldest Theological seminary are accused at this time of rationalism, and I believe the church which will not go into the heights and depths of all the truths of God as they are revealed by the Holy Spirit, is in great danger of going in the opposite direction, even to the extent of infidelity.

The promise given to Thyatira, was "He that overcometh, and keepeth my works unto the end, to him will I give power over the nations; and he shall rule them with a rod of iron; as the vessels of a potter shall they be broken to shivers; even as I received of my Father, and I will give him the morning star."

Jesus says whoever withstands the wiles of Satan shall have His power and His life with light as pure and high as the morning star. Be true to Christ and this power and light will be given to you and you will not need to search after Satan's light. With the Bible in your hand and His Spirit to teach you, you have light such as none else can give you. On every side may be unbelief and doubt and man's ideas of truth but be true to His truth, trust His Spirit and you shall go on to the greater depths and heights and be brought into the fulness of life.

V.

The message to the Church at Sardis is the darkest picture of all. It had had a name to live and was dead. It is a dark and terrible picture of complete corruption. Its place in history is in the six and seven centuries known as the Dark Ages when there was no light anywhere. Darkness had settled down on the false forms of religion, and the cold spirit of death was in the so-called Christian communities. There was no springing up into power and life. Many Christians today live in the midst of such surroundings. Jesus says they can be overcome, and a bright and glorious testimony given in spite of them.

"He that overcometh, the same shall be clothed in white raiment; and I will not blot out His name out of the book of life, but I will confess his name before my Father, and before his angels."

He says nothing to excuse though all around is discouraging and depressing. We are to stand firmly all reproach for the name of Jesus. There were a few even

255

in Sardis who had done this. Oh it is blessed to overcome and be true in the midst of uncongenial influences. The hardest times in our lives are the times when the greatest grace, and blessing and power are poured upon us.

VI.

To the Church of Philadelphia our Saviour says nothing but words of praise and encouragement. It was a church of peculiar weakness, it had only a little strength but that had been faithfully used and devoted to God. That was all, but it was enough to win a glorious promise. Though weakness itself it was made a pillar in the temple of God, and had written upon it the name of God, yes Christ said "my new name." It was given the place of known and power and glory and blessing, because here it had used its little strength for God. Are there any here that have not any strength, and whose way seems closed up? The Lord says He will open the door, and you may bear His very name and glory before the eyes of men. The little ones, the feeble ones, God uses most gloriously, those who have not many talents, but who use what they have to His honor and praise.

VII.

The last of these pictures is the Church of Laodicea. It is like the church of today, with plenty of riches and genius and talent and resources of every kind. It said "I am rich and increased with goods and have need of nothing, while God looked on and saw nothing but self-confidence and indolence and pride. He says "you are miserable and poor and blind and naked you are lukewarm and I will spew you out of my mouth," and yet at the door of this church Jesus stands and knocks. What a picture. A church, influential, proud and self-
256

confident, with a heart so full of herself that she has no room for the Saviour, and the dear master does not know whether to spew her out of His mouth or to kneel down and weep. What does He do? He pleads with her a little longer, and gives her the greatest promise of all if she will only take it. He is very near. Oh Church of Laodicea, with heart so full of other things, He is very near, but when He comes remember He has a sharp two-edged sword, and you shall not be able to set aside its retribution.

The picture of this church is very much like the first one given. In both the heart is wrong, one from decay of love, the other so devoted to culture and respectability that it become lukewarm. Why was the church in this condition? Because Christ was not in the heart, and apathy had crept over it like the pestilence, a chill like the cerements of burial. What is to be done? Wake up, shake off these garments, prepare to meet the Lord. It is just at this time He says His coming is near at hand.

This is the last picture of the church. He has told of seven battlefields on which we are to triumph. He has told us of the danger of losing heart love, of the fire of persecution we are to meet, of the attractions of the world, of the wiles of the devil, of the death of spiritual life around us, of the power of a little strength, and the last age of Christianity is indifference and self satisfaction.

And even "while He speaks He's near." "O shall you have confidence before Him, or be ashamed at his coming."

VIEW OF PATMOS,

CHAPTER XXIII.

CHRISTIAN LIFE IN THE APOCALYPSE
PART II. – THE SEVEN BEATITUDES

---

*T*HE OLD TESTAMENT closes with the word curse. The New Testament begins in the Sermon on the Mount with a blessing, and it closes with seven beatitudes in this last book. We will take them in what may perhaps be the most natural order, although any order will be instructive.

I.

"Blessed is he that readeth and they that hear the words of this prophecy and keep those things that are written therein: for the time is at hand." – Rev. 1:3.

A benediction is pronounced especially on those who study this last message of Christ to the church. There is nothing said of the danger of misinterpreting prophecy, or of the possibility of venturing into things mysterious and dark. We have been cautioned from childhood against looking too closely into these things. On the contrary, a blessing is pronounced on those who study and love it, in dependence on the Holy Spirit for guidance, who hear and read and keep the words of the prophecy of this book. I am afraid this blessing has been lost to a good many. It is quite common to hear the expression "I don't pretend to understand this book, and I don't expect to. I leave it to those who have special light about it."

This last book of the New Testament was given by Christ after the apostles had passed away, and it was given above all others to the centuries since the apostles, and particularly to the time near the end. As a mariner near shore needs to understand the shoals, and rocks near the port, so this book is written for the time near the close of the age. There are difficulties in it. The purest sterns are generally hid in the hardest kind of rock, and the sweetest kernels are found in the hardest shells. It is written in parables that the careless may not understand, but the humble may, without fear of being misinformed, if they study the book in faith, taking simply its plain literal sense. Then there will be no more trouble with it than with any other book. Blessed are they that read and continue to read it.

II.

"Behold I come quickly: blessed is he that keepeth the sayings of the prophecy of this book." – Rev. 21:7.

This is not a benediction on the hearer, simply as a general student of prophecy. It is on those who have read, and having come to a close study, have understood it, and with a keen sense of their responsibility have earnestly consecrated themselves to keep the sayings of the book. It is full of practical directions about daily life. Perhaps no book in the Bible looks more searchingly into this. In the first of the book, in the letters to the seven churches in Asia, Christ is represented with eyes as a flame of fire, searching as He passes through the midst of the church. It is an intensely practical picture. He is searching to see if His people are separated from spiritual evil from fear of suffering, from the love of the world, whether they are discouraged by weakness, are willing to suffer death for Him, or whether they need to be awakened out of the sleep of Laodicea. As the book goes on there are solemn warnings to watch and keep the garments lest the soul walk naked, also to be ready for the signs of His coming, and for His coming itself. There are special warnings given about His coming, and it is our business to be ready for it.

260

III.

"Blessed are they that do His commandments, that they may have right to the tree of life, and may enter in through the gates into the city." – Rev. 22:14.

At first sight this looks like earning our place in Heaven, but in looking at the Revised Version we see the wording is changed a little and justly changed. The error was made by some old transcriber who thought the text expressed a little too much free grace and not enough of works, and so he helped the gospel out a little by changing the reading. The two expressions, "Do His commandments," and "Wash the robes," are nearly the same in the Greek, with the exception of one letter in each word. The old MSS. read, "Blessed are they that wash their robes, that they may have right," etc. This gives the true sense of the gospel. This blessing cannot possibly be received by any one who is not living a truly sanctified life, such as the whole New Testament is constantly unfolding. The requirement for this admits of no exception, and we must have a heart which has Christ within it to enable us to do so. It is the same old gospel of cleansing through the life blood of Jesus Christ. In one of the earlier chapters of Revelation we have the same thought. "These are they who came out of great tribulation and have washed their robes and made them white in the blood of the Lamb." So in this later vision of the bride and preparation for the coming of the bridegroom, we find the same thought. The doctrine of cleansing through the blood is ever kept prominent in this book. The Lamb is the central figure. Washing the robes means not only pardon but the cleansing of the whole life. Blessed are they that wash their robes, and constantly keep them in the fountain, and so are always white and clean.

IV.

Blessed is he that watcheth and keepeth his garments, lest he walk naked, and they see his shame. – Rev. 16:15

It is not enough to wash the robes; we must also watch the robes. They must not only be cleansed, but we must watch to see they do not become stained. "Behold I come as a thief." Jesus was about to appear and steal away His people. They would be withdrawn in silence and the world would scarcely know where they were gone. By some glorious process they were carried away, but only those who were ready were taken. John tells us something of the surroundings and accompanying events of the time when this shall occur, and they are the same as the time in which we live. "I saw three unclean spirits like frogs come out of the mouth of the dragon." "They are the spirits of devils working miracles." Undoubtedly these are the demon forms of evil that are going throughout the world today, spiritualism, socialism, horrible evil of all kinds. The spirit of evil is sweeting over the world in defiance of God's word and authority, and Christ's warning is to His people that they keep their garments on. They are not merely to have their own character right but to have the divine garments on. The order is peremptory. It seems almost as if they are to sleep with the garments on, almost as if they are to sleep in the attitude of watchfulness. The foolish virgins slept without being ready, and they could not go in to the marriage. And so He says, "Watch, for ye know neither the day nor the hour wherein the Son of Man cometh."

Again there is given a beatitude for those who die in this hope.

V.

"Blessed are the dead which die in the Lord from henceforth; yea, saith the Spirit, that they may rest from

262

their labors; and their works do follow them." – Rev 14: 13.

They are not going to be excluded who die, and in the semblance of sleep rest from their irksome fatiguing labor, but their works, glad, holy, good works follow them. On earth these still live on till Jesus comes and gathers them up. They are happy now, consciously so, but they will not receive the fulness of their reward till we get ours. We know they are blessed now, at rest and conscious, and when He comes they will be made perfect. If we die before that event we shall wait for it too, so that whether we watch with the living or sleep with the glorified dead we shall all be reunited to share the glory when he comes.

VI.

"Blessed are they that are called unto the marriage supper of the Lamb." – Rev. 19:9.

These are not the dead, but the living when He comes. It includes also all who die in this blessed hope and all who are wedded in spirit to the Bridegroom and are robed and waiting for His coming. To the marriage supper of the Lamb, they are called as the bride. In the passage just before it is spoken of as being near; "and his wife hath made herself ready, and to her was granted that she should be arrayed in fine linen, clean and white." They were given to her as a gracious grant, robes white and clean, even Christ's own personal purity. Then comes the blessed fulfillment of the promise of His coming. John saw heaven opened and a white horse, and he that sat on him was Jesus, and the armies of heaven, a great procession, followed Him on white horses. The bride came behind the glorious leader, and angels and the whole universe looked on. Was there ever such a happy sight. It is worthwhile to know trial here to sit there side by side with Jesus on that day.

263

There must first come the bond of love. The name Ishi, husband, must be learned here; we must know of taking Christ into the very being; we must hear his voice not falling on a cold ear, but breathing into our very spirit. We must be taken into an intense union with Him. He says, "I have betrothed thee unto me in righteousness." There is no experience yonder, but is first had here, we will find no joy there that did not begin here. The blessed consummation, the thrill of joy and love we must know in part at least here. When all is dark and trying around us if we can know His secret voice to turn our darkness into day, what must it to be untrammeled and free in the sunlight of His presence, like a bird that has burst the bars of its cage and flown away into the infinitude of heaven. Blessed are they who know Jesus in this way. Do you know this joy dear friends or is this all sentimental talk, idle words with little meaning to you? Do you know of drawing near to the secret place and being conscious of touching something real, even His own great heart of love? You are satisfied then, everything that distracts is taken away, swallowed up in rest, and the sacred rapture of His love. What is the meaning of these wonderful expressions running through the Bible if they do not point forward to such an experience here?

"I have loved thee with an everlasting love; therefore with loving kindness have I drawn thee."

What is the meaning of this cry? I remember thee, the kindness of thy youth, the love of thine espousals."

What is the meaning of this? "I am my beloved's, and my beloved is mine."

What is the meaning of the rapturous view of the Lord Jesus Christ in the glorious vision of Hosea? What is the meaning of these and many other similar passages if they do not point forward to that joy of joys, that love of loves, that day of days the marriage supper of the Lamb. Blessed are they who are called to it.

264

"Blessed and holy is he that hath part in the first resurrection: on such the second death hath no power, but they shall be priests of God and of Christ, and shall reign with him a thousand years." – Rev. 20:6.

This is the resurrection of the dead who died in the Lord, and also a blessed vision of the translation of his children who did not die but who put on immortality in a moment and they together sat down on the throne of the millennial world. All who read Revelation with a candid mind will be compelled to acknowledge there are two resurrections spoken of there, one of the holy and another of the unholy.

The millennium closes with a terrible sight, the throne of judgment is set the throne of terror, the great and terrible day of the Lord in sight of the very smoke and fire of the pit. But His beloved ones have escaped that judgment. The first resurrection may be even now impending, how near we cannot tell, no man can tell. If the scenes around us can be taken as any forewarning the end cannot be far distant. This is the resurrection Paul speaks of in Philippians 3:11, the resurrection from among the dead. It is an elect or select resurrection, gathering up God's chosen and redeemed ones. Blessed and holy is he that hath part in it, the unholy have no part there. They slumber on in the unclean grave, they lie there in corruption till called to that terrible bar. But the blessed ones are entering into the promise that they shall live and reign with Christ a thousand years. They are beyond all suffering, all sin, all trial that could arise from their mortal frame. All tears are wiped away, Satan is bound, and they are with the personal Christ and see Him as He is. They are blessed because they can serve at His side and know of the fulfillment of plans which have been baffled here. They are blessed because there is no prospect on the other side of separation, no thought of the grave, or of the break death must bring at last. There is no dark tomorrow.

> "Life's exile hast all told its broken story,
>   Night, death and evil gone,
>   This more than Egypt shame exchanged for Canaan glory
>   And the bright City won.

Blessed are they that shall share these glorious benedictions.

CHAPTER XIV

COMPLETE IN HIM

"Christ is all and in all." – Col. 3:11.

WE are very clearly taught two great principles respecting our life in Christ, viz.:

1. That it is a NEW life, not in any sense an improvement or purification of our old life, not a training of it to better aims and sanctifying it by a sanctified end, but a new creation, utterly born from above, formed out of the resurrection life of Christ Himself.

2. That it is a PERSONAL life. It is not so much a state created in us as the union of a Person with us, the entrance of a Person into us, the life of another, even Christ Himself imparted to us, so that we can say "I live, yet not I, but Christ liveth in me." There is yet another principle to be added:

3. *It* is a COMPLETE life. It is completely wrought out by Him, and provided in Him, so that in receiving Him we receive all. Wrapped up in Him is full provision for our every possible need, nay, each detail of our future life, ready to be imparted to us as the need arises. Just as in London you can see set up the complete iron church which months later is to be set up section by section, in Sydney, Australia; so in Christ, our ascended Lord is the complete plan of every Christian's future, and it comes to us in experience as we daily need and draw upon it.

But there is so much more in Him for us than most of us draw, and the sad result often is that we are like that Church in Sydney would appear if part of the structure had been lost on the way or left ignorantly in the lumber yard, and it stood with timbers lacking and bolts left out

267

and ornaments unfinished and a general appearance of neglect and incompleteness. But why should it be so? "How much is there for us in Christ's wondrous life? What is the *breadth*, of His great love?

I. – HE IS OUR COMPLETE JUSTIFICATION.

"He hath finished transgression and made an end of sin and brought in everlasting righteousness." Once in the end of the world hath He appeared to put away sin by the sacrifice of Himself. "And being made perfect He has become the author of eternal salvation to all them that obey Him." "For by one offering he hath perfected forever all them that are sanctified." His atonement has perfectly satisfied all claims against us on account of sin. His Righteousness has perfectly met all the demands of God's holy law. His salvation is given unconditionally, freely, and forever to all that simply accept Christ Himself as a present Saviour. So that the moment the soul can say "In Christ" it can add. "Perfectly saved," "No condemnation," "No Separation."

Dear friends, are we completely justified, and do we fully recognize it and live in the light of His perfect favor?

II. – CHRIST IS OUR COMPLETE SANCTIFICATION.

This is perfectly provided for all the redeemed. "We are sanctified through the offering of the body of Jesus Christ once for all. "Of Him are ye in Christ Jesus, who of God is made unto you wisdom, righteousness, SANCTIFICATION and redemption." Here Christ is expressly declared to be Himself our Sanctification. That means a great deal more than for Him to be our sanctifier. He might be the latter and only work a subjective change in us; but when He is called our

268

Sanctification it implies the transfer to our soul of His own holiness, and the implanting and developing in us of His own pure and perfect life. Were He our Sanctifier only, the work might be slow and long because of the materials dealt with, but if He is our sanctification the work is complete the moment He Himself enters the heart. He does not have to produce in us a long, slow progeny of graces, but He brings His own abundant graces and puts them all at our service forever, and having Him we have "all things that pertain to life and godliness."

Have we received Him as our Sanctifier and are we receiving daily of his fulness, "even grace for grace?"

III. – CHRIST IS OUR FAITH.

The most vital and essential of all our spiritual qualities is faith, for it is the very link that brings us into contact with all there is in Christ, and it is the link also by which we continue in all His blessings. Nothing therefore is more important to the spiritual equipment of the consecrated believer, and nothing is more unnatural to man's evil heart of unbelief. And yet our first attempts to believe are usually made in the strength of our own natural heart. We expect Christ to do all the rest, but the faith is supposed to be our part. Nay this, too, He is willing to give. So fully does His life become our own that we live by the faith of the Son of God who loved us and gave himself for us. And this is a complete faith. This faith and this alone is adequate to all the needs of our Christian life. It requires a Divine faith to meet divine promises, to take hold of supernatural strength and to overcome superhuman adversaries. Such is the faith God expects of us, unwavering confidence, steadfast unto the end, and such faith the Lord Jesus brings unto the heart in which He reigns. Have we received Him thus as the author and Finisher of our Faith?

IV. – CHRIST IS OUR PERFECT LOVE.

Now God claims perfect love from His redeemed children, and yet in themselves they cannot render it; and how many of them all their lives excuse their coldness and selfishness as an unavoidable misfortune. But surely His grace will grant what His will requires. Yes "herein is our love made perfect, because as He is so are we also in this world." Our love becomes perfect by receiving Him, and then as He is so are we also. His love becomes our love. His heart beats in our heart. His joy flows in us, and our joy is full. His peace rests in us, and our peace is like a river, and our whole HEART LIFE becomes complete in Him.

V. – CHRIST IS OUR POWER TO WILL.

There is no element of the mind where we more need a divine regulating principle of force than the will. It is the helm of life. Its first great need is to be rightly directed, its next to be divinely strengthened. The Lord Jesus does both, He gently wins us with His love and then inclines us by His Spirit to choose His will and to become the echo of His will. His great Covenant is that He will put His laws into our hearts and cause us to choose His ways, and that He will work in us "to will and to do of His good pleasure." It is so blessed to be conscious of a life within us, spontaneously choosing with all the strength of His own will the things which He chooses and commands. And it is so blessed to be conscious of the power to grasp and hold His great and precious promises with a tenacity and strength which are nothing less than God's own omnipotence within us. Have we thus received our complete Saviour as the very spring of our life and power?

VI. – CHRIST IS OUR MIND LIFE.

Man is a threefold being, spirit, soul and body. Every part needs to be completely renewed. Corresponding to
270

these three departments of our nature, we find in the Lord Jesus the same humanity. He grew, (the physical), waxed strong in spirit (the spiritual), filled with wisdom, (the intellectual) and the grace of God was upon Him, God's blessing on all. Now this mind life of Jesus is for us as much as His spirit life, His faith, or His love. He is God's *Wisdom*, and He is made unto us wisdom. We need this as much as the rest. Our natural mind cannot rightly apprehend spiritual things. We must have Christ's mind to understand Christ's thoughts, just as we must have a man's mind to understand a man's thoughts. The fatal mistake of the past ages was to try to understand God by the light of the natural reason. The fatal mistake of the church has been to attempt to understand and teach the things of God by a merely cultivated intellect. Paul declares, "We are not sufficient to think anything as of ourselves, but our sufficiency is of God, who hath made us able ministers of the New Testament." Christ told His apostles that He would be their mouth and wisdom. Paul constantly prayed for utterance, and spake not with the words of man's wisdom but with the demonstration of the spirit and of power. Peter says "if any man speak let him speak as the oracles of God." O, what new vigor, clearness, force and freshness would possess their minds, how mightily the humblest would be used for the service of the Master and the truth, and how quickly would all our excuses if incompetency and inability be silenced if we but realized this great enduements as our right and went forth to serve Him with his own resources of all sufficient wisdom and power!

VII. – CHRIST IS OUR PHYSICAL LIFE.

1. *Old Testament Preparation.* As we look down the Old Testament, we see the clearest intimations of God's claiming the body as the object of His redeeming care.

271

We see it in the Mosaic ORDINANCES. The very first act of God after the redemption from Egypt was to announce Himself as their Healer and give them the promise of exemption from disease. They had just left the land of medical science, and if human skill was to be relied upon anywhere it was there. But they were taught from the beginning to look to God alone as their life and the length of their days. Then if God had designed to give them a better system of remedies He never had a better opportunity than when He established the Levitical system. In that, every detail of human life and every professional class was carefully regulated by positive precept and ordinance, and yet we find no remedies or physicians.

Again we see the same lesson in the EXPERIENCES of the Old Testament. Job, Miriam, Abimeleck, David, Hezekiah Asa all point to God only as the Healer and besides them there is no single case of treatment in the least analogous to modern medicine. Besides, we have the PROPHECIES of the Old Testament, announcing the blessings of Messiah's advent, and among them most clearly appears the ministry of bodily redemption. The Sun of righteousness shall arise with healing in his wings. The captives of the mighty shall be delivered. The inhabitant shall no more say I am sick. He shall bear our sickness carry our infirmities and heal us by His stripes.

2. *The Personal History of Jesus Himself.* The largest part of it is summed up in the words "He healed all that were sick that it might be fulfilled which was spoken by the prophet, saying Himself took our infirmities and bore our sickness." This makes it a ministry for every age, and gives us all a right to come still to the same gracious Helper – "Jesus Christ, the same yesterday and today and forever."

3. *The Atonement of Jesus.* His cross has a distinct and specific reference to our diseases. It was the bearing of
272

all our physical liabilities for sin. This He has done. He satisfied in His own body all claims against our body, and, therefore, "by His stripes we are healed." He bare our sins in His own body to the tree," and there He has left them forever.

4. *His Resurrection.* His resurrection was distinctly and directly physical. He rose from Joseph's tomb with a *perfect* body and a boundless life. And that physical life is for us as much as His spiritual life. "We are members of His body, His flesh and His bones," and "the life of Christ also is made manifest in our mortal flesh." Thus, while His cross removes our liability to disease His resurrection infuses a new and nobler life from His own living Heart.

5. *His Holy Spirit.* It is a part of His ministry to "quicken the mortal body," and then clothe it with life and power. Therefore, our bodies are the temples of the Holy Ghost. Therefore our members are yielded as instruments of righteousness unto God, and if they are filled with God's Spirit they will be lifted above the power of disease.

6. *His New Testament Promises and Ordinances.* Not only has He left us these glorious facts just referred to as foundation for our hope, but He has distinctly appointed the healing of disease in His name among His last and most imperative commands, and He has connected it with two sacred ordinances, the laying on of hands and the anointing with oil which add a still greater sanction to oil.

"These signs shall follow them that believe these things, they shall lay hands on the sick and they shall recover." "Is any man sick let him call for the elders of the church and let them pray, anointing him with oil in the name of the Lord and the prayer of faith shall save the sick and the Lord shall raise him up, and if he has committed sins they shall be forgiven him."

7. *His Works of Healing Power.* Those have not been left wanting. "They went forth and preached everywhere, the Lord working with them and confirming the word with signs following." "God also bearing them witness, both with signs and wonders and gifts of the Holy Ghost according to His own will.

Thus these works of healing are destined to have an important place as confirmations of the Word. They are not the ground of our faith, but lead us, with increased confidence, to seek for the Word of God. Such instances of healing are found in the Acts of the Apostles and the records of the early church. Both Irenæes and Tertullian refer freely to similar examples in their day – the second century. And as late as the fifth century there are some wonderful examples of miraculous power in Northern Africa, attested by the highest historical evidence. In the past fifty years the labors of Dorothea Trudel, Pastor Blumhardt and others in Europe and America have multiplied these instances by thousands and tens of thousands; and he who, in the light of these facts, covers almost every variety of case, can still question, may well question his own power to settle any question of truth and evidence.

Thus have we hastily sketched these seven grounds of proof for Christ s healing power and promise, and now let us merge it in the larger theme, and look once more at the greater magnitude of His entire completeness. Like the monarch of earth's mountains, which we have to look at in separate pictures ere we comprehend the majesty and magnificence of the whole, so we have looked at the different sides of Christ's fullness. We have seen Him as our Justification, our Sanctification, our Faith, our Love, our Will, our Mind, our Life.

Now let us gaze on Him as our ALL IN ALL.

1. And as we do so we rejoice in the symmetry of the picture, the many-sidedness of Christ. So let us ever view Him, receive Him and reflect Him, avoiding

274

religious hobbies, holding each truth in its relative place, and especially recognizing the Gospel of physical redemption as but a subordinate part of a greater system of spiritual truth and life, of which Jesus is Himself the center. Thus, like the full-orbed sun, will our teachings and our lives prove the lights of the world, and men, through us, shall glorify our Father in Heaven.

2. Let us rejoice in the glorious rest of such a salvation. Called not to attain, but to receive – not to struggle, but to triumph – not to give, but to take – not to make our tale of bricks without straw, but to take our pound and spend it wisely for Him – to have nothing and yet possess all things, unable even to think anything as of ourselves, and yet able to do all things through Christ that strengtheneth us.

3. Let us realize the infinite responsibility of such an opportunity – such resources – such a Christ. Who henceforth can hide away behind incompetency or unworthiness? All the resources are provided. All the sufficiency of God is at our hand. Woe to the faithless servant who neglects so great salvation. Woe to the slothful Christian who comes short of so great an Inheritance.

Made in the USA
Middletown, DE
27 October 2021